D0811016

MYSTERIES, LEGENDS, AND UNEXPLAINED PHENOMENA

SHAMANISM

MYSTERIES, LEGENDS, AND UNEXPLAINED PHENOMENA

Astrology and Divination

Bigfoot, Yeti, and Other Ape-Men

ESP, Psychokinesis, and Psychics

Ghosts and Haunted Places

Lake and Sea Monsters

Shamanism

UFOs and Aliens

Vampires

Werewolves

Witches and Wiccans

MYSTERIES, LEGENDS, AND UNEXPLAINED PHENOMENA

SHAMANISM

ROBERT M. PLACE

Consulting Editor: Rosemary Ellen Guiley

SHAMANISM

Chelsea House
An imprint of Infobase Publishing
132 West 31st Street
New York NY 10001

Library of Congress Cataloging-in-Publication Data
Place, Robert Michael.
Shamanism / Robert M. Place ; consulting editor, Rosemary Ellen Guiley. — 1st ed.
p. cm. — (Mysteries, legends, and unexplained phenomena)
Includes bibliographical references and index.
ISBN-13: 978-0-7910-9396-2 (alk. paper)
ISBN-10: 0-7910-9396-4 (alk. paper)
1. Shamanism. I. Guiley, Rosemary. II. Title. III. Series.

BF1589.P53 2008
201'.44—dc22 2008016984

Chelsea House books are available at special discounts when purchased in bulk quantities for businesses, associations, institutions, or sales promotions. Please call our Special Sales Department in New York at (212) 967-8800 or (800) 322-8755.

You can find Chelsea House on the World Wide Web at http://www.chelseahouse.com

Text design by James Scotto-Lavino
Cover design by Ben Peterson

Printed in the United States of America

Bang EJB 10 9 8 7 6 5 4 3 2 1

This book is printed on acid-free paper.

All links and Web addresses were checked and verified to be correct at the time of publication. Because of the dynamic nature of the Web, some addresses and links may have changed since publication and may no longer be valid.

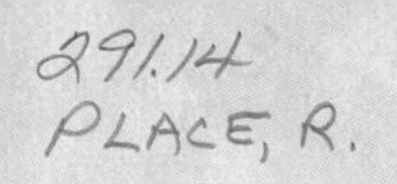

Contents

Foreword

Did you ever have an experience that turned your whole world upside down? Maybe you saw a ghost or a UFO. Perhaps you had an unusual, vivid dream that seemed real. Maybe you suddenly knew that a certain event was going to happen in the future. Or, perhaps you saw a creature or a being that did not fit the description of anything known in the natural world. At first you might have thought your imagination was playing tricks on you. Then, perhaps, you wondered about what you experienced and went looking for an explanation.

Every day and night people have experiences they can't explain. For many people these events are life changing. Their comfort zone of what they can accept as "real" is put to the test. It takes only one such experience for people to question the reality of the mysterious worlds that might exist beyond the one we live in. Perhaps you haven't encountered the unknown, but you have an intense curiosity about it. Either way, by picking up this book, you've started an adventure to explore and learn more, and you've come to the right place! The book you hold has been written by a leading expert in the paranormal—someone who understands unusual experiences and who knows the answers to your questions.

As a seeker of knowledge, you have plenty of company. Mythology, folklore, and records of the past show that human beings have had paranormal experiences throughout history. Even prehistoric cave paintings and gravesites indicate that early humans had concepts of the supernatural and of an afterlife. Humans have always sought to understand paranormal experiences and to put them into a frame of reference that makes sense to us in our daily lives. Some of the greatest minds in history have grappled with questions about the paranormal. For example, Greek philosopher Plato pondered the nature of dreams and how we "travel" during them. Isaac Newton was interested in the esoteric study of alchemy, which has magical elements, and St. Thomas Aquinas explored the nature of angels and spirits. Philosopher William James joined organizations dedicated to psychical research; and even the inventor of the light bulb, Thomas Alva Edison, wanted to build a device that could talk to the dead. More recently, physicists such as David Bohm, Stephen Hawking, William Tiller, and Michio Kaku have developed ideas that may help explain how and why paranormal phenomena happen, and neuroscience researchers like Michael Persinger have explored the nature of consciousness.

Exactly what is a paranormal experience or phenomenon? "Para" is derived from a Latin term for "beyond." So "paranormal" means "beyond normal," or things that do not fit what we experience through our five senses alone and which do not follow the laws we observe in nature and in science. Paranormal experiences and phenomena run the gamut from the awesome and marvelous, such as angels and miracles, to the downright terrifying, such as vampires and werewolves.

Paranormal experiences have been consistent throughout the ages, but explanations of them have changed as societies, cultures, and technologies have changed. For example, our ancestors were much closer to the invisible realms. In times when life was simpler, they saw, felt, and experienced other realities on a daily basis. When night fell, the darkness was thick and quiet, and it was easier to see unusual things, such as ghosts. They had no electricity to keep the night lit up. They had no media for constant communication and entertainment. Travel was difficult. They had more time to notice subtle things that were just beyond their ordinary senses. Few doubted their experiences. They accepted the invisible realms as an extension of ordinary life.

Today, we have many distractions. We are constantly busy, from the time we wake up until we go to bed. The world is full of light and noise 24 hours a day, seven days a week. We have television, the Internet, computer games, and cell phones to keep us busy, busy, busy. We are ruled by technology and science. Yet, we still have paranormal experiences very similar to those of our ancestors. Because these occurrences do not fit neatly into science and technology, many people think they are illusions, and there are plenty of skeptics always ready to debunk the paranormal and reinforce that idea.

In roughly the past 100 years, though, some scientists have studied the paranormal and attempted to find scientific evidence for it. Psychic phenomena have proven difficult to observe and measure according to scientific standards. However, lack of scientific proof does not mean paranormal experiences do not happen. Courageous scientists are still looking for bridges between science and the supernatural.

My personal experiences are behind my lifelong study of the paranormal. Like many children I had invisible playmates when I was very young, and I saw strange lights in the yard and woods that I instinctively knew were the nature spirits who lived there. Children seem to be very open to paranormal phenomena, but their ability to have these experiences often fades away as they become more involved in the outside world, or, perhaps, as adults tell them not to believe in what they experience, that it's only in their imagination. Even when I was very young, I was puzzled that other people would tell me with great authority that I did not experience what I knew I did.

A major reason for my interest in the paranormal is precognitive dreaming experienced by members of my family. Precognition means "fore knowing," or knowing the future. My mother had a lot of psychic experiences, including dreams of future events. As a teen it seemed amazing to me that dreams could show us the future. I was determined to learn more about this and to have such dreams myself. I found books that explained extrasensory perception, the knowing of information beyond the five senses. I learned about dreams and experimented with them. I taught myself to visit distant places in my dreams and to notice details about them that I could later verify in the physical world. I learned how to send people telepathic messages in dreams and how to receive messages in dreams. Every night became an exciting adventure.

Those interests led me to other areas of the paranormal. Pretty soon I was engrossed in studying all kinds of topics. I learned different techniques for divination, including the Tarot. I learned how to meditate. I took courses to develop my own psychic skills, and I gave psychic readings to others. Everyone has at least some natural psychic ability and can improve it with attention and practice.

Next I turned my attention to the skies, to ufology, and what might be "out there" in space. I studied the lore of angels and fairies. I delved into the dark shadowy realm of demons and monsters. I learned the principles of real magic and spell casting. I undertook investigations of haunted places. I learned how to see auras and do energy healing. I even participated in some formal scientific laboratory experiments for telepathy.

My studies led me to have many kinds of experiences that have enriched my understanding of the paranormal. I cannot say that I can prove anything in scientific terms. It may be some time yet before science and the paranormal stop flirting with each other and really get together. Meanwhile, we can still learn a great deal from our personal experiences. At the very least, our paranormal experiences contribute to our inner wisdom. I encourage others to do the same as I do. Look first for natural explanations of strange phenomena. If natural explanations cannot be found or seem unlikely, consider paranormal explanations. Many paranormal experiences fall into a vague area, where although natural causes might exist, we simply don't know what could explain them. In that case I tell people to trust their intuition that they had a paranormal experience. Sometimes the explanation makes itself known later on.

I have concluded from my studies and experiences that invisible dimensions are layered upon our world, and that many paranormal experiences occur when there are openings between worlds. The doorways often open at unexpected times. You take a trip, visit a haunted place, or have a strange dream—and suddenly reality shifts. You get a glimpse behind the curtain that separates the ordinary from the extraordinary.

The books in this series will introduce you to these exciting and mysterious subjects. You'll learn many things that will astonish you. You'll be given lots of tips for how to explore the paranormal on your own. Paranormal investigation is a popular field, and you don't have to be a scientist or a full-time researcher to explore it. There are many things you can do in your free time. The knowledge you gain from these books will help prepare you for any unusual and unexpected experiences.

As you go deeper into your study of the paranormal, you may come up with new ideas for explanations. That's one of the appealing aspects of paranormal investigation—there is always room for bold ideas. So, keep an open and curious mind, and think big. Mysterious worlds are waiting for you!

—Rosemary Ellen Guiley

Introduction

There have always been men and women believed to have magical, special powers and whom others look up to or go to for help. In the past they have been called magicians, witch doctors, medicine men, sorcerers, or witches, but **anthropologists**—scientists who study traditional cultures—call them **shamans** and what they do shamanism. Anthropologists borrowed this name from the traditional cultures of northeastern Asia, the area known as Siberia, where it was a native name for their magicians. Anthropologists are not certain but believe it means "someone who knows or has special knowledge."

Because the term *shaman* came from Siberia and is connected to the unique religious beliefs of the native peoples there, some scholars do not like it being used to describe medicine men and women or magicians in other cultures. They say that using the term generically creates a false idea that many of the traditional cultures of the world have the same religion called *shamanism*. Of course, the ancient Europeans, the tribal people of Africa, the native people of Australia, the Native Americans, the Siberians, the Eskimos, and other peoples do not all have the same religion. Most scholars point out, however, that they do share certain similar beliefs.

They all believe that everything in the world—not just people, but animals, plants, and rocks—has a soul or spirit. Anthropologists call this belief **animism**, which is derived from the Latin word for soul, *anima*. It is sort of like saying "soulism." Animists believe everything in their world is alive and has a hidden aspect that can only be seen if a person goes into a special trance.

A shaman performs at an international music festival in Siberia in July 2004., (Ilya Naymushin/Reuters/Corbis)

In all of these traditional cultures, certain men and women use their natural talent and training to go into a trancelike state and communicate with the spirits. They do this to help the people of their tribes and villages in various ways, and because of this they are highly valued in their cultures. These are the people called *shamans.* Shamanism, in general, refers to this religious practice, not to a specific religion.

THE VALUE OF SHAMANISM

The practice of Shamanism is very old. Prehistoric humans living in caves 40,000 years ago are believed to have practiced it, and maybe even people before that. Yet shamanism is also continually new. Shamans have continued to practice in traditional or tribal cultures around the world right up to the present. In the late twentieth century, shamanism became part of the modern New Age movement in Western culture, and some shamanic practices have been adopted by modern **psychotherapists**. There must be a reason that shamanism has been around this long and is still valued.

In the recent past Western culture with its sophisticated, technology and scientific understanding of the world has tended to view traditional cultures as primitive and backward. Modern anthropologists, however, have come to appreciate that these traditional peoples have their wisdom. Often, traditional cultures have an appreciation of the workings of nature and how to exist in harmony with their surroundings. Similarly the shamans in these cultures understand human nature and can teach people about their inner power and how it can be used for health and well-being.

Anthropologists realized that modern civilization has its roots in these traditional cultures and that in ancient times traditional Western cultures had shamans. As society replaced magic with science and technology and advanced its understanding of the world, however, it also lost some valuable stuff. To help recover it, some anthropologists and other modern Westerners, who were initiated into tribal

Pacifying Souls

In the 1920s, Danish explorer Knud Rasmussen asked an Iglulik Eskimo shaman living in the central Canadian arctic why the shaman's role was important to his people. The shaman told him:

> *The greatest peril of life lies in the fact that human food consists entirely of souls. All the creatures that we have to kill and eat, all those that we have to strike down and destroy to make clothes for ourselves, have souls that do not perish with the body and which therefore must be (pacified) lest they should revenge themselves on us for taking away their bodies.*[1]

The Eskimos live in a region with little vegetation. They don't have broccoli or cotton, and they rely on hunting for all of their food and clothing. They, like many other traditional peoples, believe the shaman's role is necessary for making peace in the *spirit world* and helping them get over the guilt caused by hunting as a way of life.

shamanism, began to write and teach about shamanic traditions. That is how shamanism came to be part of modern culture.

One of the things that make shamanism valuable is that unlike the group rituals of modern organized religions, shamanism is an **ecstatic** religious practice.[2] *Ecstatic* means that the shaman goes into a type of trance that is associated with ecstasy or bliss. In this trance, the shaman enters an inner world that few people are familiar with. It is a strange, dreamlike world, but the details of the structure of this world are similar in the reports of shamans from different times and places. Being in this world is something like entering a dream while awake and consciously deciding what to do there. This world is invisible to people's normal daytime mind, but to a shaman in a trance, it is just as real. Here the shaman can meet gods and animal helpers and gather magical power. Once this power is gained, the shaman can use it to make changes in the everyday visible world, such as healing the sick or making it rain.

Unlike most people in modern group religions, the shaman worships alone. The shaman can talk to God, or the gods, or even animals or plants directly, and these entities talk back. It is a path to wisdom, health, personal confidence, and other good things. Shamans in traditional cultures helped people in various ways. This is why shamanism has always been part of the human experience and why it is still drawing the interest of people in the modern world. Here are nine of the shaman's most common jobs:

1. To cure illnesses
2. To find game for the hunt
3. To divine the future
4. To interpret dreams
5. To find lost people or objects
6. To help guide the tribe
7. To appease spirits
8. To control weather, especially when rain is needed
9. To help people to feel good

Besides the benefits that shamans provide for their people, their spiritual visions are believed to be the oldest form of religious experience. It is a personal visionary religious experience not controlled by a group or an outside authority, like a priest, who presides over a ritual based on tradition and dogma. It demonstrates that religion stems from individual experiences that are natural to humans and found in all ancient and primitive cultures.

SHAMANS ARE NOT ALL THE SAME

Although there are many basic ideas about shamanism that tend to be the same in all shamanic cultures, it is important to realize that there are differences also. Each shaman has an individual experience when he or she enters a trance, which is not entirely like any other shaman's. Shamans also are continually adapting to their cultures and to the changes in society. This creates differences. The differences can be seen in the following categories:

Male Versus Female

In some cultures such as in Siberia, shamans are almost always men, although they do value the power of women, and sometimes these men even dress as women to increase their power. In Korea and among the Sora people of India, most shamans are women. In most cultures, though, a shaman may be a man or a woman.

Dress

Often shamans wear magical clothing for their work. In Siberia a male shaman may dress as a woman or wear a special leather tunic covered with bits of metal, believed to have magical properties, sewn to the outside. Traditional Mayan shamans wore elaborate ritual costumes with complex feathered headdresses. Often a shaman's power is thought to be connected with his or her costume. Modern urban shamans in Peru, however, just wear their street clothes to practice.

Tools

All shamans use tools in their work, but some need more than others. Other than their ritual dress, Siberian and Native American shamans need a drum, a rattle, and maybe a pipe for smoking herbs to help them sing themselves into a trance. In Peru and the Caribbean, however, shamans set up elaborate altars with swords, ceramic sculptures, and other magical tools.

A Mayan ceremonial sculpture of a bearded high priest, or shaman, in the jungle in Guatemala. (Charles & Josette Lenars/Corbis)

Drugs

Some shamans, particularly in Mexico and South America, use **hallucinogenic** drugs derived from herbs to help them enter a trance. Others, such as the Siberian shamans, rely just on their singing and concentration instead. Where hallucinogenic herbs are used, however, they are considered sacred and not to be abused.

The Spirit World

All shamans enter a trance where they experience an alternative reality, which may be called the spirit world, the other world, or the dream world. Australian natives, or aborigines, call it the *dreamtime*. This alternative reality is remarkably similar in all shamanic traditions, and most shamans travel through this inner landscape to meet helpers who increase their power. There are some shamans, however, who sit still in their trance and invite the helpers to travel to them. This is particularly true in Africa and African-based shamanism in the Americas where the spirits enter and possess the shaman.

Feeling Good or Ecstatic

A shamanic trance is referred to as an ecstatic state of consciousness. Ecstatic is related to the word *ecstasy* and this makes it sound like shamans are feeling really good when they are in a trance. This is true some of the time, but shamans also deal with some scary spirits at times, particularly in the Lower World and the realm of the dead. Therefore, shamanic trances can also cause overwhelming fear. When people are called to shamanism but decide not to do it, it is usually because they cannot handle the fear that they will have to experience.

Helpers and Teachers

All shamans get help from people and animals in the dream world. These helpers can be guides who increase the shaman's power or teachers who basically teach shamanism. In different cultures, however, the guides and teachers are different. They can be animals, spirits, or gods from the myths of the culture that the shaman lives in. In Brazil and the Caribbean, for example, shamans often have Christian angels or saints for helpers.

Doing Good

Most shamans are men and women who enter a trance to gain power to help their people through healing, providing direction, helping people work in harmony, and other good things. In many cultures, however, there are shamans who want only to gain power to help themselves. There are even shamans who want to cause illness and generally do bad things. Some anthropologists prefer to call these negative shamans *sorcerers* or *black magicians* instead of shamans.

This book will not teach readers how to become a shaman, but it will explain a lot about shamanism. It will discuss the history of shamanism from prehistory to the New Age and the various forms shamanism has taken in different cultures. The book will not only explain what shamans do and what tools they use, and delve into their worldview, but it will also describe shamanistic experiences and at times let the shamans explain themselves. It will also discuss how shamanism is used in modern culture.

The History of Shamanism

More than 20,000 years ago in what is now southern France, Dahma lived alone in her hut. It consisted of a dome of wooden supports anchored at the bottom by a short wall of stones and covered with the hides of several bison, expertly stitched to fit the form and painted with the image of she-bear, a symbol of her power. In the center was a circle of stones, which contained a fire, and the smoke drifted up through the hole at the top of the dome. Dahma was part of a village, but her hut was outside of the circular cluster of the villagers' huts. She lived alone outside of the circle because her power was too great for others to live near her. She was the shaman who watched over her people.

Dahma rose at sunrise and prayed to the morning star because today she had important things to do and she needed the star on her side. The tribe's hunters had not seen a herd of bison for several months, and they knew they would not find any unless Dahma could capture the soul of the bison and bind it to the clan. Dahma washed in the spring near her hut, donned her finest deerskin tunic with a fringe of antler carvings dangling from the neck, grabbed her bag of tools, and began her trek up the mountain. Despite her limp, which was the result of her **initiation** and a sign of her power, Dahma walked swiftly. About a mile up the slope, where she had a good view of the valley and the village, Dahma found the entrance to the sacred cave where shamans such as herself had been coming for the past 10,000 years. Dahma stopped and took a soapstone lamp out of her bag. She filled the hollow bowl of the lamp with a combination of animal fat and tree resin and placed a wad of fine dry grass on top. Then she used her sparking flints to ignite it. With the lamp lit she entered the cave.

Deep inside one of chambers that branched off the main shaft, Dahma began her work. She knew that she was in the right place because the walls and ceiling were covered with paintings of animals. She used the flame of her lamp to ignite a small pile of hardwood kindling that she had brought with her and stacked in a fireplace that was hollowed from the rock. Then she placed the lamp on a rock ledge. In front of the fire she unrolled the skin that contained the various red and yellow ochers and other dark minerals such as manganese that she used for her paintings. Minerals are basically rocks of different colors, and Dahma's were ground into a powder and mixed with fat and resin to form large crayons that were easy to use. Dahma, however, had work to do before the drawing could begin. She took the rest of her tools out of her bag and just sat.

Dahma threw sacred herbs on the fire. Then she sat and chanted in front of the fire, swaying back and forth to the sound of her leather drum for a long time, long enough to begin to see the inner world. The chant was a prayer that called the soul of the bison to her. As she chanted, Dahma saw with her closed eyes that the soul of the bison was rising from deep within the womb of the Earth to meet her in this chamber. When she felt it was near, she opened her eyes and there she saw it, in profile, as big as life, in a clear space high on the wall of the cave.

Dahma placed some sticks in the holes cut in the side of the cave to form steps for her to climb. She grabbed her lamp and her black manganese crayon, climbed the steps, and began to trace the figure of the soul. She started with the tail and continued to the head, drawing a sharp outline and then blending the black into the background where needed. Then she colored it with some red and some yellow blended together.

Figure 1.1 *Detail of a bison head from the Paleolithic mural painting series in Lascaux, France.,* (Pierre Vauthey/Corbis Sygma)

WHERE IT STARTS

Shamanism seems to be as old as the human race. Archaeologists, scientists who study prehistoric people, tell us that the first human ancestors who looked and thought like us, ***Homo sapiens***, lived in Africa 130,000 years ago. From there they traveled and settled all over the world. About 40,000 years ago, humans settled in what is now Europe and created cave paintings, engravings on bone and antler, antler and stone carvings, clay sculptures, and other artifacts that have lasted into modern times. Also, they probably created a lot of things that did not last because they were made out of perishable materials such as wood, leather, or plant fibers. There is some evidence for some of this, but for the most part scientists can only guess at what these things looked like. This period, when early humans lived in Europe, is called the Upper **Paleolithic** Epoch, which means the newest part of the Old Stone Age. It is called the *Stone Age* because the people from that time used stone to make tools and art. Even the paints they used for the cave paintings were made of ground-up stone.

The artifacts they left behind says much about early humans' religious beliefs. For example, they buried their dead in the earth covered in red ocher with jewelry and tools. The tools they made sometimes had animals or symbols carved on them that seem to have had more than a decorative function. They left a lot of paintings of animals deep in caves where they did not live and therefore could not be thought of as decorating the home. Some of these paintings are of creatures that have a combination of parts from different animals, the kind of figures found in mythology or in the trances of shamans.

Because they did not leave any written records of their thoughts, what these ancient people believed is not exactly known. They made their living by hunting for meat and fish and gathering herbs and fruits. Traditional or primitive cultures of hunter-gatherers living in the world today have animistic beliefs. They are concerned with the souls of the animals that they hunt, and they have traditions of shamanism. So it is seen as likely that Stone Age people also had a shamanistic

The Wizard on the Trois Frères Cave Wall

In 1910 the cave of the Trois Frères, meaning the cave of the three brothers, was discovered in France, by three brothers. The cave contained some paintings of bison and other subjects dating from 13,000 BCE. The most famous painting in the cave, however, is one called the Dancing Sorcerer. By the title, Sorcerer, the *archaeologists* were referring to a shaman. The Sorcerer is a human figure with deer antlers, bear claws, and a horse's tail. Although no one knows whether it was meant to depict a shaman in animal dress or a god that is actually part human and part animal, the Sorcerer is obviously magical. It is either a shaman or related to the kinds of visions that shamans have. It is one of the best bits of evidence that ancient people practiced shamanism.

Figure 1.2 *An artwork rendering of the so-called Dancing Sorcerer cave painting from circa 13,000 BCE in Les Trois Frères cave system.* (Charles Walker/Topham/The Image Works)

tradition that was connected to hunting magic. The story that opens this chapter is fictional, but it is based on modern shamanistic practices and incorporates archaeological evidence of shelters, tools, and art left by early Europeans.

Some modern scholars do not like to make guesses about the practices of prehistoric people, and if they cannot know for certain, they prefer to say nothing. The influential scholar of religion Mircea Eliade (1907–1986), however, points out that to say nothing gives the false impression that our ancestors had no religion and this can lead to a worse misunderstanding.[3] Making guesses can be a good thing as long as the guesses fit all of the facts and don't leave any of them out, because if the guess does not fit the facts, it cannot be true.

A 40,000-YEAR TRADITION

Most prehistoric shamanism seems to have been concerned with magic for hunting, but these shamans were also the first artists and the first doctors, and some of their art suggests other magical pursuits. The traditions of the shamans who made the cave paintings in western Europe lasted for about 20,000 years. In comparison, written history began only in the Bronze Age, about 5,000 years ago. The culture of the ancient Egyptians seems far removed from the present, yet the first cave painter was even further removed in time from the last cave painter, four times as long as the Egyptians are removed from today.

About 10,000 years ago humans entered the **Neolithic**, or New Stone Age, Period. Instead of living in small groups and relying on hunting and gathering for food, many humans began to raise animals and crops on farms and store food. Then larger groups of people could live together in villages. Shamans adapted to these changes and began to work for the needs of the new groups, such as performing rituals for weather magic to help the crops or performing group healing or healing for animals. They did not lose their tradition of hunting magic, but added these new skills to their list of things they could do.

In this period, a new type of religion started in which people performed group rituals guided by priests. Priests were the first alternative to shamans and in some ways they were rivals for authority. In contrast to the intuitive spontaneous visions of the shamans that were always changing, the priests worshiped specific gods and told stories about them, called *myths*, which would remain basically the same over time. Here again the Neolithic shamans adapted, and the gods and myths of the priests began to be incorporated into their trances. At times the roles of shaman and of priest were mixed, and one person could be both.

The next great change in human culture started about 6,000 years ago and continues to the present. This was the **Urban Revolution**, in which large groups of people left farms to live in cities, where they could specialize in certain crafts and exchange their goods for those of farmers or craftspeople. Some shamans migrated to cities as well and began to work on urban needs, especially health, love, and prosperity, but again they maintained the skills and beliefs that they had learned as hunters and as farmers and added to this body of knowledge. Like potters, carpenters, and other tradespeople in the city, shamans were thought of as craftspeople. Farmer and hunter-gatherer cultures, however, continued to exist, and shamans continued to thrive in these more traditional cultures.

With cities came the rise of civilization and organized religion, and priests became more powerful. In some cultures, such as in traditional Tibet, shamans and priests took care of their separate roles and lived in harmony influencing each other. In other cultures, such as among the Mayans of Central America and Mexico, the role of the priest and shaman merged into a sort of shaman/priest. In still other instances, however, priests began to see shamans as threats to their authority. This is what happened in Western culture when Christianity developed. As Christianity spread through Europe, shamans were condemned and persecuted as devil worshipers, although they do not believe in the Christian Devil. During this time shamanism tended to disappear in Europe.

Beginning in the 1400s Europeans built ships that could sail across oceans, and they began to travel around the world trading for goods and setting up colonies. This is called the **Age of Exploration**, and it lasted from the 1400s to the 1600s. Although shamanism no longer existed in most of Europe, Western Europeans now came into contact with shamans from other cultures. At first they saw shamans as a threat and condemned them as devil worshipers, just as they had done in Europe. They tried to convert them to Christianity or destroy them.

In the 1700s, which is called the **Age of Enlightenment**, Europeans began to develop modern science, and scientific-minded explorers began to see that shamans were representatives of other, more primitive religions. Because of their scientific skepticism, however, they tended not to believe in the magical powers that shamans claimed to have. Many of these scientific-minded Europeans and people of European backgrounds who were now living in America and other colonies decided that shamans must be scam artists or con men who took advantage of superstitious people who lived in primitive societies. People in Western culture, although trying to be more enlightened, still believed that traditional people lived the way they did because they were naive or unenlightened, and that the shamans, being the smartest people in those cultures, took advantage of the others by making outrageous claims about their power.

One of the sciences that developed in the 1700s was the study and comparison of human cultures, or anthropology. Because anthropologists attempted to understand culture without prejudice or preconceptions, they began to see the important role that shamans played in their cultures. It took a long time for them to overcome prejudicial ideas, though. Even in the 1900s modern psychologists working with anthropologists thought that shamans must be crazy people who managed to serve some purpose in their cultures.

In this period, however, psychoanalyst Carl Jung (1875–1961) began to appreciate the depth of wisdom found in the human unconscious. This appreciation led him and his followers to study shamanism as

Figure 1.3 *A hand-colored print of a Native American shaman based on an 1832 painting by George Catlin.,* (The Gallery Collection/Corbis)

a traditional exploration of the same area. Jung developed a healing psychological technique called active imagination that is an exploration of the dreamlike landscape of the unconscious mind while one is awake and able to interact with this vision. It is very similar to a shamanic trance. Later, other psychologists incorporated shamanic practices into their work. And this interaction between shamanism and psychology continues to evolve under the title of *active imagination* or ***journeywork***.

In the 1950s, perhaps because of Jung's influence, anthropologists began to actually listen to shamans and participate in their rituals. Then they began to appreciate that shamans were skilled at entering an alternative state of consciousness and that their work had psychological benefits, particularly for healing. They saw that shamans practiced folk medicine in contrast to the biological medicine practiced by modern Western doctors. Eliade was the first scholar to fully appreciate shamanism as a form of religion and help other people to understand it. He was a scholar of religion who was influenced by Jungian psychology and who wrote *Shamanism: Archaic Techniques of Ecstasy*, which was published in 1951 and defined shamanism for other scholars and scientists.

NEOSHAMANISM COMES TO THE UNITED STATES

In the late 1950s and in the 1960s, many people in Western countries became unhappy with the lack of spirituality they saw in Western culture. When they read about shamans from traditional cultures, they wanted to learn more about their practices and experience these altered states of consciousness for themselves. One of the most influential articles was "Seeking the Magic Mushroom" by R. Gordon Wasson (1898–1986), published in *Life* magazine in 1957. Wasson pointed out that Mexican shamans ate a certain mushroom, which was hallucinogenic and helped them to alter their consciousness. Many people in the West, who were already experimenting with hallucinogenic drugs, also became interested in shamanism. Many of these people began to visit Mexico and experiment with mushrooms and some of the other hallucinogenic herbs used by shamans. Using drugs for fun, however, is dangerous and not the same thing as using them as shamans do to alter their consciousness and enter a state of mind where they can heal people.

In the 1960s books by Carlos Castaneda (1925–1998) became popular. In his books, Castaneda wrote about his experiences using drugs to alter his consciousness and gain shamanic power under the guidance of a Mexican Indian shaman named don Juan. Many people doubt the truthfulness of his accounts and even doubt whether don Juan existed. His critics suggest that he was a con artist making up sensational stories and saying they were true to make money, but Castaneda did include some factual information about shamanism in his books, and he did a great deal to popularize shamanism in English-speaking countries.

By the 1980s anthropologists who had been studying with shamans for many years began publishing popular books about shamanism. One of the most influential was Michael Harner, who had been studying with shamans in the Amazon jungle in the 1950s. In 1980 he published *The Way of the Shaman*, in which he not only spoke about his experiences but began to teach people traditional shamanic techniques for going into a trance without drugs. By combining techniques from many traditions, Harner developed a course in shamanism that he began to teach at workshops around the United States. Because his technique combines practices that are from many cultures and is geared toward his American students, this form of shamanism came to be called **neoshamanism**.

While neoshamanism continues to spread through Western culture, traditional shamans continue to practice in tribal cultures around the world. Often these traditional shamans run into trouble with the authorities, who pass laws trying to stop their practice. Although many people in the West have come to appreciate the value of shamanism, shamans are not always valued in their native countries. Many developing countries where shamans are active are trying to modernize and look at shamans as being out of date.

The Shamanic Cosmology

Juan lives in Lima, Peru, and works as a carpenter part time. The rest of the time he works at one of his people's oldest professions. He is a shaman, or as he is called in his country, a ***curandero***. At one time the government and the Catholic Church tried to stop shamans from practicing, but in modern Peru shamans are a tourist attraction and good for the economy. Although their beliefs stem from ancient Incan traditions, they have made concessions to the Catholic Church and include Christian saints among their helpers and Christian symbols among their power objects.

The role of a shaman in a modern city is not the same as it was in rural villages in the past. Besides healing, Juan is often asked to help his clients succeed in business or love, or in combating city diseases such as alcoholism. Also, tourists come from distant countries and hire him for rituals. Juan is doing so well that he hopes to be able to quit carpentry soon and become a full-time *curandero*.

Today, Juan is performing a healing ritual for a local man who has been overcome with feelings of jealousy because of a neighbor's success and his own lack of success. The ritual will take all night, and some of the man's relatives will be with him for support. Juan starts at 10 p.m. by setting up his altar, called a ***mesa***, in the courtyard of the man's house. The altar is basically a table, on which Juan places a bundle covered with a handwoven cloth and unfolds it to reveal the contents. Out of the pile Juan takes a crucifix and places it in the center of the cloth on the altar to divide it into four sections, which relate to the four directions, or four winds, like a sacred map of the world. The crucifix also divides the altar in half. On the left side Juan places things representing evil, such as poisonous herbs and demonic figures. On the right he places good things, such as healing herbs and statues of saints. The center the crucifix represents a place of balance between good and evil. This is also the sacred center, and by sitting at the altar, Juan is entering that sacred place. In the sand in front of the altar, Juan places various swords and staffs that he will need in his **journey**.

The ritual will have two parts. For the first part, which will last until midnight, Juan will journey to the Lower World to cleanse the man of evil influences or spirits. In the second part, which will last until morning, Juan will travel to the Upper World to gain help, and the man will be energized and cured.

Once everyone is seated on the ground, Juan starts by praying to each of the four winds and makes offerings to each. Then he purifies the altar with a spray of perfume. To help him enter a trance, Juan prepares a hallucinogenic drink made from the **San Pedro cactus**. This is not something that Juan takes lightly. The San Pedro cactus is a sacred plant to him, and Juan had to travel many miles to the sacred mountain at Chapari, which his shamanic tradition considers the center of the world, to gather the cactus himself. After he drinks the cactus juice, Juan offers it to the man and his relatives. This is followed by a drink of black tobacco juice, which decreases anxiety and increases concentration. When used together, the drinks have a calming effect and clear everyone's minds.

Now that everyone is in the right mood. Juan uses his rattle and chants to enter the spirit world and root out the evils that have been plaguing his client. At midnight this process is complete. Next, Juan prepares a second drink of the sacred cactus juice. In the second part of the ceremony Juan uses tobacco smoke as incense to raise energy and help him ascend to the Upper World. He chants and dances, and before long he has everyone joining in. He gives each of them

Figure 2.1 *A Peruvian shaman performs a ritual.*, (Aurora/Getty Images)

one of the swords or staffs to help defeat the evil influences, and by sunrise, although they have been up all night, everyone is alert and left with a feeling of well-being from their inner journey. Juan ends the ritual by thanking the four winds and sprays everyone with a white substance made from lime juice, cornmeal, sugar, and white flowers to protect them.

THE CENTER OF THE WORLD

People sometimes get an urge to find a magic place, a place where they feel more powerful and where special things can happen, maybe on top of a certain hill, under a protective tree, or even sitting up in the tree. This is the same urge that shamans have. From the beginning of time, shamans have noticed that certain places seem better than others for magical practices, such as going into a shamanic trance and contacting the spirits. Sometimes shamans find naturally powerful spots, such as the interior of caves with prehistoric paintings found in Spain and southern France, and sometimes they can construct a power spot, as the South American shamans do when they construct their altars. Sometimes the power spot is an ordinary tree. Shamans in all cultures tend to refer to this kind of spot as the "center of the world." Sometimes scholars call it the ***axis mundi***, but that is just Latin for the "pole in the center of the world."

The idea of being in the center to the world may seem strange initially. First of all, the world is a sphere, and therefore the center is actually in its middle. This is a place that scientists call the core. It is so hot there that rock melts into lava. Shamans, however, are referring to the center of the world as a place on the surface where they can sit, and they obviously do not mean the core.

Their concept seems to be based on the idea that the surface of the world is a flat circle and that the center of the circle can be located. To find the center of this giant circle, a shaman must draw a line from the north to the south poles and then cross it with another line connecting the east pole, where the Sun comes up, with the west pole, where the Sun

Figure 2.2 *An illustration of the World Tree and the three worlds, (from top to bottom) the Upper, Middle, and Lower.,* (Robert M. Place)

sets. The place where the lines cross is the center and, in pinpointing it, the shaman has aligned him- or herself with the four directions also.

This circle divided into quarters is actually how most ancient peoples viewed the world, and it is how shamans traditionally view the world. They also believe that there is another circle below the Earth on which we live. This is the Lower World. There is also a third one above us, the Upper World above the sky. The Lower and Upper Worlds are actually invisible to humans unless they are shamans and go into a trance. Even in a trance, though, the shaman must climb down or fly up to get to one of the other worlds. The center of the world is a place where there is an opening to the other worlds and the most likely place for the shaman to make the journey.

Shamans believe that there is more than one center of the world. In some cultures, such as in Mongolia and among the Native Americans who lived on the Great Plains, every house is constructed as a model of the world, and the center of every house, where the fire is kept, is the center of the world. Yet the Sioux, a tribe of Native Americans who lived on the northern Plains, also considered the Black Hills in South Dakota as the center and, therefore, very sacred.

To understand this concept we need to examine how one perceives the Earth. Living on the surface of the ball of the Earth, people can see only so far before the Earth curves away out of sight. Therefore, the Earth always looks to us like a very large, round, flat surface. Also, because the Earth tends to curve away equally in all directions, people appear to always be in the center of this surface. Wherever one stands actually appears to be the center of the world.

When a shaman calls a spot the center of the world, he or she is really saying that this is a place where he or she becomes aware of the entire world and his or her place in it. It is a sacred place, where the shaman feels at home, centered, and oriented toward the four directions. It is more of a state of mind than a place. The reason that shamans believe that the Lower and Upper Worlds are similar to this world is that when they go there in a trance, those worlds look like this one and also curve away in a big circle. In shamanic trances the center is often marked by a tall object that seems to connect this world to the Lower and Upper ones, and shamans look for or create symbolic centers to represent this in everyday reality. A natural center could be a mountain or a large tree. One constructed by humans might be a pole or simply the column of smoke rising from a sacred fire.

THE CENTER IN WORLD MYTHOLOGY

The concept of the center of the world as a sacred place is found in nearly every mythology and religion throughout history and in every part of the world. The fact that this idea is found everywhere suggests that most modern myths and religions grew out the visions of shamans. Here are some examples of the sacred center in mythology.

In Norse mythology, the myths of the ancient Germanic peoples, the world is a lot like that of the shamans. The ancient Germans and Vikings believed that people lived on a giant, flat Earth called Midgard, which translates as "Middle Earth." In the center of Middle Earth there was a giant tree that held together nine worlds stacked one above the other. Of the nine there are three chief ones, as in the shamanic model.

The giant tree is called **Yggdrasil**, the **World Tree**. Middle Earth encircles the trunk of Yggdrasil, like a donut with the tree in the hole. Above the branches is Asgard, the home of the gods, and the most important of the Upper Worlds. Below Middle Earth, at the roots of Yggdrasil, are the underworlds, the homes of the fates and fearsome giants. Prominent among the lower worlds is Hel, the home of the dead. In the Germanic myths, Yggdrasil was the place that heroes had to get to if they wanted to travel to the other worlds like the shamans.

The Germanic model influenced the modern Christian idea that Heaven, where God lives with the good people who have died and the angels, is above Earth, and Hell, where the bad people who have died now live with the Devil, is below the Earth.

In Buddhist mythology, instead of a giant tree, the center of the world is occupied by a magical mountain, called **Mount Meru**. Besides being in the center of the world, Mount Meru is said to be shaped like a pyramid, like the ones in Egypt but bigger, and each of the four sloping sides of the mountain face directly toward one of the four directions: north, south, east, and west.

As in the shamanic visions, the center helps to orient people toward the four directions. Each side of the mountain is said to be made of a different substance: the north of gold, the east of crystal, the south of sapphire, the west of ruby. The Buddhists also associate the four sides of the Meru with other magical groups of four such as the four elements and the four seasons. Like the shamanic worlds, Mount Meru ascends through numerous worlds, from the base, which is home to the Asura, a race of scary warrior giants, to the top, where the gods live. Many levels above the land of the gods, at the very top, live the enlightened Buddhas. In Buddhism there is more than one Buddha, and they are even higher than gods.

In the Buddhist cosmology Mount Meru is found in the center of a great ocean with 12 continents equally spaced around it, and each is a different color. Humans are said to live on the blue continent to the south of the mountain. Buddhists create a type of sacred painting, called a ***mandala*** that takes the form of a circle with the center and the four directions clearly indicated. A mandala is actually a map of this sacred world view.

In Buddhist mythology, just like in shamanism, there is also more than one sacred center. According to the story of Siddhartha, the young hero who became the Buddha of the current era, he searched the world until he found the perfect place to sit in meditation and become the enlightened Buddha. It turned out that the perfect spot was under the Bodhi tree, a fig tree that grew on the axis or center of the world. So, the Buddhists actually used both a mountain and a tree to mark the center.

In other cultures, this theme is repeated wherever people need to indicate sacredness. The ancient Greeks believed that Mount Olympus, where the first Olympic Games were held, was the center of the world, but also that Delphi, with its famous Oracle who gave advice direct from the god Apollo, was the center. The Babylonians believed that Babylon or, specifically, the ziggurat, a pyramid-like structure that was in the center of the city, was the sacred center and that the gods stood on it to create the world. The Tibetans believe that Mount Kailash, in the Himalayas, is the center. In Islam, everyone is required to pray five times a day facing Mecca, which is believed to be the sacred center. To Christians, Jerusalem, Bethlehem, the Vatican, or other places that are destinations for pilgrims can be considered the sacred center.

LIVING IN A YURT

The Native Americans, the Siberians, and the Mongolians all tended to build their houses as though they were smaller versions of the world. They were round and domed or cone shaped with a fire in the center.

Figure 2.3 *Mongolian yurts in the Inner Mongolian Autonomous Region in northeastern China.,* (Liu Liqun/Corbis)

This pattern exists in the Native American tepee, the Siberian tepee, the Navajo hogan, the Apache wickiup, the eastern Native American wigwam, the Eskimo igloo, and the Mongolian **yurt**. To construct a space in this pattern is to make that space sacred—to make it a place where people are centered, conscious, and aware of their place on earth. It shows that these native peoples all wanted to live with this type of awareness.

To the Mongolians, knowing where the north, south, east, and west are located at all times is essential to one's sense of well-being and the knowledge that one is in the center. It helps them to feel at home in the world, and it is the first thing they need to know

Feng Shui

Feng shui (pronounced "fung shwee" or "fung shway") is a traditional Chinese mystical practice that seems to have its roots in ancient shamanism. The goal of feng shui is to create an aesthetically pleasing, healthy, and properly energized living space. The practice involves the arranging of architectural details, objects, shrubbery, and colors to achieve harmony with one's environment and a proper balance of a mystical psychic energy that the Chinese call ch'i (pronounced "chee"). Once a feng shui practitioner has achieved the proper balance of ch'i in a dwelling, it is believed that it will bring health, wealth, and joy to its inhabitants.

One aspect of feng shui that is comparable to shamanistic practices is the use of color to symbolically orient a dwelling to the four directions and the sacred center. The Five-Element Ba-Gua Color Wheel is a mandala-like diagram used by feng shui practitioners as a model for the proper orientation of a living space. It may also be compared to the floorplan of a yurt. The five principal colors on the color wheel are black in the north, red in the south, green in the east, white in the west, and yellow in the center.

when building a yurt. The yurt must be oriented correctly to the four directions, and each direction has symbolic significance. The most important direction, however, is the fifth, the center, which, of course, is sacred. So, building a yurt begins with constructing a circle or hoop of wood that will frame the smoke-hole in the center of the roof. Next, poles are lashed to the hoop, pointing out in all directions like the rays of the Sun. The other end of each pole will be bent and placed in the ground so that the wood structure forms a dome with the hoop at the top. The floor of the yurt is dirt, but the walls get covered with latticework and then wool felt blankets. In the far north, they are covered with animal skins.

These five colors and directions are also correlated with the five elements that are found in Chinese philosophy: water, fire, wood, metal, and earth. Between the four outer colors are found four colors that represent the diagonal directions, such as blue in the northeast.

In the center, where one would find the hearth in the yurt, there is a circle with the curved line dividing it into halves. One half is black, representing the yin feminine principle, and other is white, representing the yang masculine principle. This is a Tai Chi, one of the most sacred symbols in Chinese philosophy. Its suggested movement represents c'hi. Placed around it are eight symbols composed of groups of three broken or unbroken lines, representing yin or yang energies. These are called trigrams, and they are derived from the ancient Chinese book of **divination**, the *I Ching* (pronounced "EE jing"). In the *I Ching* these trigrams are said to represent a family with a mother, symbolized by three broken lines; a father, symbolized by three unbroken lines; three sons, symbolized by trigrams with one unbroken line and two broken; and three daughters, symbolized by trigrams with one broken line and two unbroken. This can be thought of as the family of trigrams as living in this space.

Each of the four directions has particular functions that a Mongolian living in a yurt must know. The fire is placed in the center of the yurt just below the smoke hole, the most important spot. The fire is called the daughter of the sky father. The dome of the yurt represents the dome of the sky and the rising smoke is the World Tree; the smoke-hole represents the opening to the Upper World, where the sky father lives.

Mongolians do not refer to the other four directions as north, south, east, and west. They call the south the front, like it is part of their body, and when they look out at the front, they can watch the Sun traveling across the sky. They associate the front with fire and the color red, like the Sun when it is rising. The door of the yurt must be facing the front, and movement in the yurt must always be clockwise, or in the same direction that the Sun moves, as people move around the fire.

The north is called the back. The back is associated with water and the color black. Being farthest away from the Sun, it is dark, and the rains probably come from this direction. The back of the yurt, farthest from the door, is a special spot, although not as sacred as the center. The Mongolians keep a small altar here with sacred objects and pictures of gods. When elders or honored guests come to visit, this is where they will sit.

The Mongolians call the east, where the Sun rises, the left, and this is associated with air, the color blue, and it is considered female. The left side of the yurt is where the wife in the family keeps her belongings, such as cooking pots and a cradle-board, used for holding a baby on its mother's back. She sits here and the children can sit with her. The west, or right, where the Sun sets, is associated with the element earth and the color white. It is masculine and the husband sits here. He also keeps his things here, like his saddles, bows, and guns.

If a person living in the yurt is also a shaman, the place is already set up in a sacred pattern and ready for his or her rituals. The shaman can sit on the floor near the fire drumming, and once in a trance he or she can visualize climbing up the column of smoke and ascending to the Upper World. In fact, for an initiation ceremony, a tree trunk with the branches cut short is first placed in the center of the yurt with the top of the tree sticking out of the smoke-hole. Once the drumming has taken effect, the shaman actually climbs up the tree and out the hole. At the top, the shaman transforms into a bird and flies to the Upper World. This last part is likely to be visualized by the shaman while in a trance state, but observers of this ritual have claimed that the shaman disappeared for a while after climbing out of the smoke-hole.

Shamanic Tools

Koinyt lived in a forest in Siberia. His father had been a shaman, and Koinyt grew up listening to his father telling stories about his adventures in the Other World. Besides being a healer, Koinyt's father was a good storyteller, and he used to entertain the children with his tales. His father had been dead for seven years when Koinyt learned that his father's stories were more than just entertainment. The spirits that his father had worked with started to come to Koinyt in his dreams. They told him that he was also a shaman.

Because of his dreams, Koinyt found an older shaman to teach him his father's craft, and after this apprenticeship the time came for his initiation. Before he could be initiated, Koinyt had to make his drum. The drum is the most important tool of the shaman. It is more than a musical instrument. Shamans think of it as their magic horse that will carry them to the Other World. The wood that it is made from has to come from the World Tree in the sacred center. So before Koinyt could begin to make his drum, he had to obtain some of this sacred wood. To do so, Koinyt would have some help from the spirit world.

That night, Koinyt had a dream in which he saw lightning strike the sacred tree in the center of the world. A branch fell off and landed in the forest near his cabin. In the morning Koinyt went into the forest with his ax to find the wood that the dream had promised would be there. To be sure that he was guided by the spirits and not just his eyes, Koinyt closed his eyes and walked with his hands stretched out in front of him. He passed many trees before he found himself hugging a large tree that felt right. When he opened his eyes, he saw a birch tree that had been burned by lightning. He knew it was the tree promised in his dream.

Koinyt blessed the tree by praying as he sprayed it with a combination of blood and vodka that he had brought in a bottle placed in his bag. Then, using only his ax, he began to cut out a section of the tree that was the right size for the body of his drum. The cutting took most of the day and Koinyt had to return the next day and the day after with a friend to help him before he finished the cutting and the hollowing of the drum. When it was done, Koinyt took the large wooden tube home with him. It still needed deerskin cover on the head, but that would wait until Koinyt found a sacred deer. For now he would concentrate on bringing the core of the drum to life by anointing the wood with beer and praying to the spirits.

POWER OR MAGIC OBJECTS

Besides gaining power from being in the center of the world, shamans use tools to increase their power. Shamans have a job to do. They make deals with spirits and bring help to their people by providing healing and guidance. Power is an invisible substance that strengthens a shaman's soul and helps him or her to be more effective.

Rattles and drums

The most common power objects shamans use are ones that make a repetitive sound and help the shaman to go into a trance. Shamans around the world have found that the best music to help induce a trance is a simple repetition of a strong sound. For this sound, shamans mostly use percussive musical instruments such as drums or rattles. If a shaman has no other tools, they will at least have something like this. In addition to their practical, musical use, these instruments are also magical and increase power. They may be thought of as having a life of

Figure 3.1 *This drum is used by Lapp shamans to induce a trance. The drum skin is made from reindeer hide and is decorated with pictures and symbols.,* (Tiziana and Gianni Baldizzone/Corbis)

their own and be treated as helpers. In Siberia, for example, a shaman's drum is thought of as a spirit horse or deer that the shaman can ride to the dream world.

In Siberia, where shamans rely primarily on the drum instead of a rattle, shamans will sometimes carry a steel staff to assist on his journey. The staff may be symbolic of the *axis mundi*, and it may serve as a magical weapon. It usually also has bits of metal hanging from the top and can be used as a rattle. As a Siberian shaman acquires natural and crafted power objects, mostly made of iron, he will tie these to his leather clothing until the entire tunic is covered with dangling objects and he has actually turned his whole body into a rattle.

Symbolic clothing

In Siberia the shaman's tunic may also be embroidered with a design representing the sacred World Tree. That way, as soon as he puts it on, the shaman is in the sacred center. Similar designs made with beadwork exist on Native American shamanic tunics. Another piece of power attire that we find in Siberia and the Americas, or could have found in ancient Europe, is a headdress adorned with antlers, such as the antlers on the cave painting of the Sorcerer in France mentioned in Chapter 1. The antlers may connect the shaman with the deer as a power animal, but they also symbolize the World Tree. Likewise, the feathered headdresses used by many Native American and Siberian shamans may symbolize the World Tree and also connect the shaman with the power of the bird, which will help the shaman in journeys to the Upper World.

Images of helpers

As shamans acquire teachers and helpers from the dream world, they make or collect objects that represent these allies. Often these are simple figures—carved of wood, stone, or clay—of the gods, ancestors, or animals that serve as allies. The figures, however, are more than mere statues. Some shamans believe that the images can come to life and perform magical tasks for them. They may even swallow them to gain the power of the ally.

Because shamans wish to identify with their allies and merge with them, animal costumes are popular. Wooden masks are used for this purpose in Africa, in the South Pacific Islands, and among the Native Americans. Many shamanic objects of this type, especially masks, are sought by art collectors, but to the shaman their value is more than artistic. In the Amazon jungle where most shamans identify with the jaguar, they may even tattoo their faces with jaguar markings and pierce their noses and add whiskers.

Altars

Besides using clothing to get centered, a shaman may use objects to create a map of the world with the four directions and the sacred center

Figure 3.2 *Wooden Eskimo figure representing the spirit of an ally. In this case, the ally is a nineteenth-century Greenlandic shaman.* (Werner Forman/Corbis)

clearly depicted. Often the traditional house serves this function, but if a shaman doesn't live in yurt or a tepee, he or she may need to create something to get centered. One way to do this is to construct an altar. These are popular with shamans in Peru and in Africa. Almost any box or table can serve as an altar. The important thing is to align it with the four directions: north, south, east, and west. That way, when the shaman is at the altar, it is clear that he or she is in the center.

Besides power objects representing allies, Shamans place objects representing the four elements in the appropriate areas of the altar to help orient it. These can be natural objects such as a rock to represent earth, a crystal to represent water, incense to represent fire, or a feather to represent air. Each of these would be placed to the north, south, east, or west, but the element that is associated with each direction differs depending on the shamanic tradition.

Mandalas

Besides creating an altar, a shaman may create an art object such as a painting that represents the sacred map of the world depicting the four directions and the sacred center. Scholars tend to refer to these designs by their Hindu and Buddhist name, *mandala*. One example of this is the **god's eye** made by South American shamans. The god's eye is made of two or four sticks tied together in a cross with colored yarn woven over them to form a symmetrical design radiating toward the four directions. Another is the **sand painting**, which is a circular design made of colored sand carefully placed on the ground by a Navajo shaman. In the Navajo healing ritual, the patient actually sits in the center of the sand painting, which brings them back to the center and to health.

MAGIC HERBS

Besides getting help from animals, gods, and ancestors, shamans get a lot of help from the plant world. One of the most sacred symbols in shamanism is the World Tree, which is actually a giant plant, but besides this, shamans make use of a variety of herbs in their work. The shamanic use of herbs falls into three categories.

Herbs for Healing

Healing is one of the main concerns of shamans, and besides getting help from the spirits, shamans have used the practical approach of herbal medicine to heal their patients for thousands of years. All traditional cultures around the world use plants for healing, and it seems that they always have. In all of these cultures shamans are the experts in the use of herbs.

Figure 3.3 *A Navajo shaman making a sand painting.* (Danny Lehman/Corbis)

Anthropologists tell us that our ancient ancestors who painted in the cave in Lascaux, France, depicted the use of herbs in their paintings up to 25,000 years ago. There is also evidence that the Neanderthals, the prehistoric people who existed before modern humans, used herbs 60,000 years ago. There are thousands of herbs that are used by different cultures for healing. About 25 percent of the drugs used in modern Western medicine are derived from herbs. For example, the common drug aspirin was originally derived from the herb willow bark, the herb that Black Elk used in his pipe (see box, Black Elk's Sacred Pipe).

Even animals seem to intuitively choose certain plants to eat when they are feeling sick, and anthropologists guess that people first learned about herbs by watching animals. Shamans say that they sometimes learn about herbs from animals. Like animals, however, people have the intuitive ability to find herbs. Shamans report that they are also guided to plants by their **spirit guides**, and that they sometimes talk to the plants themselves to find what they need.

Healing herbs can be used in foods, drunk as a tea, applied to the outside of the body, or even smoked in a pipe, as is popular with Native American shamans, such as Black Elk.

Symbolic Herbs

Besides using herbs directly for their medicinal effects, shamans also use herbs for their magical powers. One of the most common ways is to burn the herbs as incense. Incense is often burned because it smells good, like perfume, but to a shaman incense is used in rituals to help him or her enter a trance or to attract certain spirits. It seems that some spirits like some smells more than others. If a shaman can get a spirit's favorite smell, he or she can count on its help.

Black Elk's Sacred Pipe

In 1930 on Pine Ridge Reservation in South Dakota, author John G. Neihardt interviewed Black Elk (1863–1950), a shaman of the Lakota Sioux tribe. Neihardt recorded Black Elk's life story, but before Black Elk began he wanted his biographer to understand the importance of his most sacred tool, his pipe. The following excerpt from Neihardt's account records Black Elk's words:

> So I know that it is a good thing I am going to do; and because no good thing can be done by man alone, I will first make an offering and send a voice to the Spirit of the World, that it may help me to be true. See, I fill this sacred pipe with the bark of the red willow; but before we smoke it, you must see how it is made and what it means. These four ribbons hanging here on the stem are the four quarters of the universe. The black one is for the west where thunder beings live to send us rain; the white one for the north, whence comes the great white cleaning wind; the red one

Incense has been used since ancient times by shamans. During the Neolithic Period (10,000 years ago) it was adopted by priests to help create the right atmosphere for group rituals. In Christian rituals, for the past 2,000 years, the tree resins frankincense and myrrh have been used for incense. These herbs were used as incense even before Christianity started and were valued for their ability to help mystics concentrate and get into a trance. Perhaps they were first used by shamans.

Sometimes incense can be used for healing. Among Tibetan shamans, all incense is believed to have healing properties and may contain combinations of up to 30 herbs, such as juniper, clove, cinnamon, and other good-smelling herbs. One of the most common uses of herbs among neoshamans in the Native American tradition is as a purifying

> for the east, whence springs the light and where the morning star lives to give men wisdom; the yellow for the south, whence come the summer and the power to grow.
>
> But these four spirits are only one Spirit after all, and this eagle feather here is for that One, which is like a father, and also it is for the thoughts of men that should rise high as eagles do. Is not the sky a father and the earth a mother, and are we not, all living things with feet or wings or roots, their children? And this hide upon the mouthpiece here, which should be bison hide, is for the earth from whence we came.[4]

Black Elk's pipe, like other shamanic tools, is richly layered with symbolism connecting it to the four directions and to one sacred presence. The symbolism of the pipe turns it into a mandala, an object that represents the sacred map of the world, the four directions, and the sacred center. When Black Elk smokes his pipe, he is automatically in the sacred center. The specific relationships between the directions and the colors, however, are not identical in the various shamanic traditions.

smoke that is healing and sets the right atmosphere for shamanic work. For this they will burn a **smudge stick**, which is a bundle of sage, an aromatic grass, tied together with yarn. This seems to be derived from a practice of Native American tribes of the plains.

Herbs Can Be Dangerous

Although shamans respectfully use mind-altering drugs derived from herbs as an aid in their work, these entheogens, as they are called as a group, can be harmful to one's physical or mental health. The most physically harmful drugs that the shamans use, surprisingly, are the ones that seem the most common—nicotine, derived from tobacco, and caffeine, derived from coffee. Nicotine is more addictive than heroin, and its habitual use has been linked to cancer, birth defects, and heart disease. While caffeine is less harmful than nicotine, used in large amounts, as shamans use it, it is hallucinogenic; causes dependency, severe nervousness, and anxiety; and in some individuals can lead to psychosis.

While psilocybin, the active ingredient in psilocybin mushrooms, has half the physical toxicity of caffeine, it is an illegal hallucinogen that can impair judgment and may cause severe anxiety or trigger psychosis. Mescaline, the drug derived from the peyote cactus in the Southwestern United States and Mexico and from the San Pedro cactus and the Peruvian torch cactus in South America, is also of low toxicity but highly hallucinogenic. The same precautions apply to it as with psilocybin.

Mescaline has been illegal in the United States since 1970 and internationally since 1971. The law, however, does not apply to mescaline's use as a sacrament in Native American religion. The law seems to recognize that in religious or shamanic practice, these drugs are used more safely because of the ritual structure that accompanies their use.

Besides incense, herbs may be included in a magical amulet or talisman. This could take the form of a leather pouch, called a medicine bundle by Native Americans, which is filled with herbs and other power objects and worn to gain power or for protection. Similar bags were made by African Bantu shamans, and the tradition was brought to the United States by the African slaves in the 1700s and 1800s. They are still used by African-American hoodoo magicians today in the form of a felt bag, called a mojo, containing herbs, a lucky coin, a lodestone, or other ingredients.

Symbolic magical herbs may also be used as one of the objects placed on an altar to add to its power. Peruvian shamans, for example, include many herbs on their altars, not just the ones needed for the ritual they are performing at that time. On the right of the altar, they may place healing herbs, and on the left, poisonous herbs, to add to the energy of the altar and represent good and evil.

Herbs for Changing Consciousness

Most shamans rely on repetitive music and concentration to enter a trance, or sometimes fasting and lack of sleep. In some areas, however, particularly in the Americas, shamans also use hallucinogenic herbs to help them enter a trance. In southern Mexico the Native American shamans eat hallucinogenic mushrooms called **psilocybin mushrooms**. When this discovery was written about in *Life* magazine in the 1950s, it created a stir in the public imagination and, for better or worse, helped to popularize shamanism.

Peruvian shamans use the San Pedro cactus to help them enter a trance. In the Southwestern part of the United States, Native American shamans use **peyote cactus** as part of their sacred sweat lodge ceremony. Both plants contain mescaline, which is a psychoactive substance (one that alters a user's perceptions and consciousness). There are, however, about 100 different herbs used by shamans to alter their state of mind.

Shamans used these herbs as an aid in their healing rituals and not as party drugs. They consider these herbs sacred and mostly do not misuse them. Actually, although it is not a hallucinogen, the most common herb that Native Americans use to alter their consciousness in both North and South America is tobacco, which helps one to temporally feel relaxed, calm, and yet alert. Shamans do not tend to smoke tobacco as a bad habit. They use it as a sacred herb only during their ritual, where they may use a lot of it all at once. Besides smoking it as a huge cigar, a shaman may also chew the leaves, inhale it as powder, or drink it as juice. Another common herb used by shamans to alter consciousness is coffee, which energizes one and increases alertness. They may make it stronger than most people would want to drink with breakfast, and they may use a lot of it at once.

All shamanic tools, in any tradition, whether they are clothing, musical instruments, or herbs, are carefully selected and designed to enhance the shaman's power and help the shaman to enter an ecstatic trance. In some traditions shamanic tools are skillfully made works of art, and in others they may be found objects that are adapted to the shaman's purpose. The obtainment of one's tools, however, is always a serious matter that involves intuitive insight and ritual.

The Initiation

Henry was born in 1885 into the Washo tribe of Native Americans living around Lake Tahoe, Nevada. Henry's father ran away when Henry was three years old, and Henry lived with his mother, who was a servant on a ranch in Genoa, Nevada. They were poor. Henry spent most of his time alone, wandering through the ranch and surrounding countryside. As a child he did not speak English, and the only people he could talk to were members of his tribe.

Although Henry did not have a father, he idolized his uncle, Welewkushkush, who was a great healing shaman. Henry would watch as his uncle chanted and entered his patients' houses to do his healing. Henry also had an older sister, who was married, and her husband, Henry's brother-in-law, was a shaman who could sing antlered animals to sleep and make it easy for the hunters to find them.

When Henry was nine years old, he went to live at a school run by white men. Here he had to learn English and become a Christian. Speaking his tribal language and making any mention of his traditional beliefs were grounds for punishment. This was the time that the spirits chose to contact Henry.

Sleeping in the school dormitory, Henry had a bunk like everyone else in the large room. One night, however, he was visited in his dreams by a great bear that looked like it could eat him. The bear stared at him for a while and then vanished. Henry was not frightened by the bear, and when the bear suddenly vanished, Henry flew up into the sky to look for him. He did not find the bear, but his search led him to the Moon, where he met other helper spirits.

The next night Henry had a similar dream, and again the night after that. Although he could not talk about it with anyone, Henry realized that he was going to be a shaman like his uncle.[5]

RECEIVING THE CALL

A shaman is someone with a talent for going into a trance and dealing with the spirit world. Becoming a shaman also takes a lot of training. In certain places, such as parts of Siberia, shamans are rare, but in others, such as the Amazon jungle, many people are shamans. They are not, however, all equally powerful. Power is one of the things that sets a shaman apart from other people and determines how successful he or she will be. Therefore, a shaman must know that he or she has some power before asking to be initiated.

In Siberia a shaman may inherit his power from his father. The son of a shaman grows up seeing many things that his father does and hearing the stories of his father's shamanic journeys. He is effectively being trained from birth to be a shaman, but that does not mean all children with a shaman parent will become shamans. Some of the shaman's sons will not want to be shamans. Many people believe that a shaman inherits his or her power before birth regardless of whether the child comes from a line of shamans or not, and it takes time for the child to grow and realize his or her power.

The Native Americans living in the prairie traditionally sent all young men of a certain age out into the wilderness to fast and pray for several days and gain a vision of what their life would be about. This is called a *vision quest*. The ones who were going to be shamans would know from their vision. Among the Sora, a traditional people who live on the east coast of India, shamans are mostly women, who although they are married to a human husband have a spirit husband as well. The shaman's spirit husband proposes to her in a dream or vision.

Her son fathered by her spirit husband, living in the spirit world, will marry a human girl who will become a shaman of her line. In most cultures a shaman does not actually choose to become a shaman; it is the spirits that choose the shaman.

Once the spirits have chosen someone to become a shaman, they visit the person in a dream and ask them to play, to be their lover, or begin to teach. The dreams will naturally increase the shaman's power, and most people respond to the call.

Sometimes, however, the process is not painless. The future shaman may fall ill and become delirious. While in this forced trance, the future shaman will go into the spirit world and learn about illness and how to cure it. He or she will then cure him- or herself. Often the shaman suffers from an illness that would kill most people, such as smallpox, but the shaman is cured and gains the power to cure others. In Siberia the illness often takes a particular form that people

Figure 4.1 *Greg Red Elk performs a reenactment of the Sioux vision quest of a shaman.* (Marilyn Angel Wynn/Nativestock Pictures/Corbis)

recognize as a call to shamanism. It is a type of madness in which the sufferer is plagued by demons.

Once the shaman realizes that he or she is a shaman, it is necessary to seek out a teacher and eventually be initiated into his or her full power.

THE INITIATION

The first part of the shamanic initiation is instruction. A shaman who receives the call from the spirit world may seek out one or more older shamans as teachers and start an apprenticeship. If a shaman comes from a family of shamans, a parent or another relative may teach him or her. The Lakota shaman Black Elk, discussed in Chapter 3, was trained as a boy by all 11 shamans of his tribe. This was unusual, but the shamans worried that their tradition was dying and wanted to make sure they passed it on to someone with talent. Some shamans, such as those in the upper Amazon forest, actually pay for instruction or power, but this is rare. The best teachers are the spirits themselves.

When the Siberian shaman enters into the shamanic sickness, or when the spirits come to a young shaman in dreams, or a young Native American on a vision quest receives a vision of a power animal or guide, they are already beginning their instruction and initiation. No matter what training the shaman receives, the ultimate initiation is actually the first journey into the spirit world. This initiation will involve a change in the would-be shaman's personality as the old ego or self-image is let go of and a new stronger and wiser personality emerges. This is not necessarily a pleasant process.

The initiations described by Siberian shamans and some Eskimo shamans seem more like horror movies than descriptions of a blissful trance. The spirits come to the would-be shaman in a vision and tear apart his body until there is nothing left but a skeleton. Even his head is removed. It seems like he is being tortured by demons, but these spirits are actually his allies or friends.

Next they begin to rebuild his body, and as they do, they install new strengths and abilities. The shaman's eyes may be cut out, but new eyes that can see into the inner secrets of nature and understand the language of animals or plants are installed. The shaman's body may be cut up and boiled in a pot, but when it is cooked it will be put back together with the ability to cure illness. The head might be cut off and hammered by a blacksmith, heated and tempered, and put back on the body better than new with strength and wisdom. This type of initiation can be terrifying, but in the end, the shaman comes back to normal reality feeling blissful and better than ever.

All shamanic initiations involve a death of the old self and a birth of the new, but they are not all as horrific as the Siberian version. A young Sora shaman may face some frightening characters in her dreams as she is learning, but her life transformation happens when

The Way of Suffering

The Danish explorer Knud Rasmussen, who interviewed Eskimo shamans, asked one named Igjugarjuk where shamanic power comes from. Here is his answer:

> All true wisdom is only to be learned far from the dwellings of men, out in the great solitudes; and is only to be attained through suffering. Privation and suffering are the only things that can open the mind of man to those things which are hidden from others.[6]

Just as Native American shamans must fast in the desert to find their vision and Siberian shamans must pass through the shamanic sickness to gain spirit helpers, Igjugarjuk had found that to become a shaman it is necessary to remove oneself from distraction and face one's inner fears. Only by conquering these inner demons does one gain power. In some traditions, however, this does not have to be a painful process.

she marries her spirit husband. After the marriage she is able to go into a trance at will and talk with spirits. Some shamans actually experience the initiation as a vision of rebirth. They return to the womb of the earth mother and are reborn. This can also take the form of being swallowed by a giant animal such as a bear, a snake, or even a fish, such

A Siberian Shaman Describes His Initiation

In the 1930s the Siberian shaman Dyukhade was asked by an anthropologist how he became a shaman. He said:

> Before she became pregnant, my mother had a dream in which she became the wife of the Smallpox Spirit. She woke and told her family that her future child was to become a shaman through this spirit. When I grew up a little I fell ill for three years. During this illness I was escorted through various dark places where I was thrown into water, now into fire. At the end of the third year I was dead to the world and lay motionless for three days. It was only on the third day that I woke up again, when they were getting ready to bury me. During those three days, while the people around me thought I was dead, I went through my initiation. I reached the middle of the sea and heard a voice saying "You will receive your gift from the Master of the Water. Your shamanic name will be Loon (a diving bird)."[7]

After this, Loon came out of the water and saw the Mistress of the Water lying on the beach. Then he became her son. Although some of his learning experiences were scary, his initiation, unlike many Siberian initiations, was not. It was a return to the womb in the form of the sea and then a rebirth as the son of the Mistress of the Water. Like all initiations it was a death of his old self and the birth of his new shamanic self.

as in the story of Jonah, and then being thrown up or reborn from the animal. The Native American on a vision quest breaks away from his old self by fasting and praying in the desert or the wilderness. The new self will come in the form of a vision of a power animal that will be his spirit guide and friend from then on. The guide teaches the shaman what to put in his medicine bag and what songs to sing to call on the spirits when he needs to.

Some of the unpleasant experiences during the initiation can be chalked up to a beginning shaman's inexperience. Once the shaman has gained knowledge, power, and spirit helpers, he or she is not as vulnerable and is ready to return to the spirit world to battle the demons that cause illness or to find lost souls. This is called *journeying.* It is the primary thing that a shaman does.

Shamanic Journeys

Sumbari lives in the jungle in Orissa, on the east coast of India. She is a shaman of the traditional Sora people. In her language she is called a ***kuran***. Sumbari has eaten no food this morning because she is fasting, but she did have a strong drink containing some alcohol. She is preparing for a journey into the spirit world. The purpose of this journey is to contact her ancestors and gain knowledge that will help in her practice.

To start the journey Sumbari's assistant lights the clay oil lamp, the form of which Sumbari inherited from the spirits. It has a figure of her monkey helper sculpted on the edge, the same animal that helped the shaman who taught Sumbari. With the lamp lit, Sumbari will be able to see into the underworld, the place that she calls the "murky-sun country." Next, Sumbari sits on the floor with her legs straight in front of her, closes her eyes, and beats a steady rhythm on the floor with a knife. As the beat takes over, she begins to sing a song that calls on her monkey spirit guide, other spirit helpers, the souls of the deceased, and former shamans from her line. Her journey is one that normal people can take only when they die because it is to the land of the dead. A kuran such as Sumbari, however, can leave her body and make the journey while still alive. More importantly, she can also return to the land of the living.

Middle Earth and the lower murky-sun country are connected by the World Tree, and although the journey is treacherous and steep,

Sumbari must climb down the tree. To accomplish this she calls on her agile spirit guide. The monkey not only comes to Sumbari but enters her, and she sees herself transformed into the likeness of her helper. Now she can scamper down the tree with ease. As she descends through the misty border between this world and the lower one, she stops singing in the conscious world and her chin drops to her chest. Sumbari has arrived in the underworld, where she may communicate with the spirits. Her assistant, sitting near her silent body, awaits Sumbari's return.[8]

JOURNEYING

A shamanic journey is not like going to the beach for the day or visiting another city. It is not a vacation. It is an inner journey into a world that is more like a fairy tale than ordinary reality. To explain it in psychological terms, it is an adventure into the inner unconscious world of the mind.

The shamanic map of the spiritual world is actually a map of the human mind, or psyche. There shamans can meet forces or personalities in their unconscious and work with them to fix things in their mind. Swiss psychologist Carl Jung called these forces or inner personalities the **archetypes**. Some of these archetypes are hostile, but others are natural helpers and guides.

During an inner journey, some of the threatening archetypes that initially attack can be transformed into allies. This seems to happen in the Siberian initiation when the shaman befriends the forces of disease that at first cut him up and reassemble him. In the end they become his friends and help him to cure illness.

One of the main ways a shaman cures illness is by finding lost parts of the soul while on a journey and bringing them back to their owners. In psychological terms, losing part of one's soul seems similar to what psychologists call **dissociation**, in which a person cuts off part of his or her personality or psyche and suffers depression or illness because of it. Usually dissociation is caused by bad things happening to someone. Like a healing shaman, to cure the patient, the psychologist has to return the lost parts to their owner.

When a shaman journeys, he or she will most often visit one of the three worlds and meet teachers and allies who will help him or her gain power or fight and bargain with the demons of illness or other spirits, while looking for lost souls. A shaman may visit the future or another planet, but for the most part shamans journey to one of the three worlds. Each of these worlds may not just be a single land but may actually be made of numerous layers. A shaman can explore any of these layers.

THE MIDDLE WORLD

Humans live in the Middle World or Middle Earth in normal consciousness. Therefore, it might seem that a shaman would start here

Returning a Soul Through an Ear

The pioneer of the study of shamanism, Mircea Eliade, provided the following description of a Siberian shaman of the Tremyugan people healing his patient by finding a lost soul part. Notice that besides a drum the shaman uses a guitar.

> The Tremyugan shaman begins by beating his drum and playing his guitar until he falls into ecstasy. Abandoning his body, his soul enters the Underworld and goes in search of the patient's soul. He persuades the dead to let him bring it back to earth by promising them a gift of a shirt or other things; sometimes, however, he is obliged to use more forcible means. When he wakes from his ecstasy the shaman has the patient's soul in his closed right hand and replaces it in the body through the right ear.[9]

and only journey to the Upper or Lower Worlds. When a shaman journeys to Middle Earth, however, he or she sees it in a different way. The shaman sees the spiritual aspects of the earth and uses the journey in Middle Earth to do the spirit work that needs to be done here. A shaman may communicate with the spirits of rocks, trees, and other plants, or the entire Earth, personified as the Great Mother; he or she may travel to the four directions to gain power from the spirits of the four elements or the four seasons; or he or she may make a journey to the sacred center such as a sacred mountain or the World Tree.

A shaman journeying in Middle Earth may even travel to the Moon. To a shaman, the moon is not part of the Upper World, which is actually above the sky, the Moon, and the stars. Some shamans, such as the shamans of the Nenets, traditional people who live in northern Russia, are actually afraid of the Sun and the Moon. Their shamans fear that if they fly too close, they will be trapped there, which they believe is what happened to the Man in the Moon, who is an important figure in their mythology.

One advantage of a journey to Middle Earth is that the shaman is already there. Once a shaman enters a trance, he or she can begin exploring. In a trance, however, the shaman can move quickly, even fly the way people can in a dream, which makes traveling in Middle Earth a lot easier than it normally would be. Shamans often take advantage of this and use journeys to Middle Earth to visit far-away places, to heal the sick in a faraway villages, or to look for animals for the hunt or lost objects.

In Middle Earth a shaman meets spirits of nature, such as the spirits of plants. This type of journey is an opportunity to talk to plants and learn about herbs. The shaman also meets the spirits of animals. This is one of the most important reasons for journeying in Middle Earth. A shaman cannot be a shaman for very long unless he or she gets help from the spirit world, and the first and most important helper to the shaman is the spirit guide, also known as the guardian spirit or power animal. Spirit guides or guardians are mostly animal spirits, which live in Middle Earth or in the Lower World.

A beginning shaman usually visits either of these worlds first and looks for his or her guide. A spirit guide teaches the shaman power songs, provides power objects, leads the way on other journeys, and protects the shaman from danger. It is the shaman's principal ally and teacher. Many cultures believe that even nonshamans have them but are unable to see and work with them like a shaman. A guide or guardian may even take on human form. They are similar to guardian angels in modern Western religions.

The anthropologist and shamanic teacher Michael Harner said that a shaman knows when he or she is chosen by a spirit guide because the spirit will present itself to the shaman four times so that four sides will be seen. For example, it may appear in profile facing left, appear from the rear to show its back, appear facing right, and then appear facing forward.[10] This ritual behavior is related to the four directions, as though the spirit is honoring each direction before it presents itself. Other sure giveaways are that the guide is friendly, helpful, and even if it is an animal, it is able to talk to the shaman. A shaman may have more than one spirit guide. Sometimes one will leave and be replaced by another. Spirit guides are also known for their sense of humor and their habit of playing tricks, particularly to outsmart an enemy.

In addition to animal helpers, other helpers and teachers may be the souls of former shamans. The shaman may encounter unfriendly ghosts as well as ones in need of help, such as ghosts that have been unable to leave the earth plane for the land of the dead. A shaman may help these ghosts by guiding them to their home. Certain shamans tend to specialize in this work, acting as **psychopomps**. The word *psychopomp* comes from Greek for soul, *psyche*, plus guide, *pomp*, and means soul-guide. In Middle Earth the shaman may also run into other problem spirits, similar to the troublesome fairies of Celtic tradition, but it is the Lower World that has a reputation for being less friendly.

THE LOWER WORLD

Because the Lower World is also a good place to find an animal guide or guardian, it is a popular first journey for young shamans. Shamans consider the Earth the mother of creation and believe it can be good place to return to the womb and experience the rebirth of the initiation. More than any other world, however, the Lower World, or Underworld, is potentially threatening and can even be deadly. Many cultures think of the Lower World as the dimly lit home of the dead. To journey there is to travel the route that the soul travels after death. For example, the Sora shamans of India warn that if a shaman journeys there, she should not eat any food that is offered because this is the food of the dead, and it will bind her to the land of the dead so that she cannot return. Also, she should not play with the children there because they will likewise bind her.[11]

The initiations of Siberian shamans tend to take place in the Lower World. This is also the land of the spirits that cause illness, and some of them participate in the initiations in a frightful way. These associations with death and illness are the very reason a healing shaman needs to go there. Shamans journey to the Lower World to be initiated and to find animal guides and allies among the spirits of illness that will help them to heal those illnesses. They also go to the land of the dead to talk with departed ancestors, who may be important teachers and who can teach them about the past. Additionally, they go to the land of the dead to find lost souls or to do battle with the spirits of illness or other demons from the Lower World that have captured a soul.

To get to the Lower World, a shaman can go to the World Tree and climb down to its roots as Sumbari did. Almost any natural opening into the earth can work, however, such as the caves that the prehistoric people of Europe used to paint in, or a spring or steam that goes underground. Often shamans will visualize themselves diving into a well, a water hole, or even a hollow tree trunk. The shaman can also follow an animal helper into the earth, especially one that naturally burrows into the earth, such as a mouse, a snake, a woodchuck, or a rabbit. This is one reason why it is good to find an animal guide as soon as possible. Often, to keep the animal guide close, the shaman regularly sees him- or herself turning into the animal, as Sumbari did with her monkey. This is helpful for journeying because then the shaman has the same powers and abilities as the helper. Modern shamans who are familiar with modern inventions, such as the city shamans of Peru, may just use an elevator to journey into the earth.

Whatever doorway to the Lower World a shaman chooses, once it is entered the shaman finds him- or herself descending a tunnel or shaft that may contain some hidden dangers. Once the shaman comes out of the shaft, he or she finds that the Lower World is not that different from Middle Earth, maybe just a little darker. There are land, sky, trees, and mountains just like on Middle Earth. All three worlds share this quality, even the Upper World.

One of Us Has to Die

A modern Western man with a New Age view of shamanism remarked to a Nepalese shaman, "How good it must be to live in harmony with the cosmos." The shaman answered, "The main part of my job is killing witches and sorcerers (his names for enemy spirits). I am terrified every time before I perform a big ritual because I know that each time, one of us has to die."[12]

As one can see by this example, the traditional shaman does not always share the New Age view of his profession. To the traditional shaman, a journey to the shamanic world can be fraught with danger and can be life threatening, while to the modern Western man in the story, it seemed to be a romantic adventure. The difference in their viewpoints lies in the fact the modern Westerner thinks of the shamanic world as a fantasy, and the traditional shaman experiences it as another aspect of reality.

THE UPPER WORLD

The Upper World is above the sky in the Middle World, and it has ground and sky just like Middle Earth, but it tends to be brighter there with more sunlight. To get there a shaman can climb the World Tree, a sacred mountain, a rainbow, or even the smoke rising through the smoke-hole of his dwelling. Once he or she climbs above the Moon and the sky, he or she will come to a barrier, perhaps made of clouds. In Siberia the barrier is made of ice, and the Shaman must hack through it. Spectators actually say that they have seen and felt the ice falling as the shaman cuts it away. When the shaman breaks through the barrier he or she enters the Upper World.

Another method for getting to the Upper World is flying. The shaman may have the power to fly, but most often the power comes from an ally, particularly one with wings such as a bird or a butterfly. To do this, the shaman may transform into his or her winged ally or ride on its back. Also, some allies, such as the spirits of deer, seem able to carry the shaman to the Upper World without wings. Another method of flying is a strong wind that carries the shaman into the air. This wind can also take the form of a tornado that sweeps the shaman up. The Native American shamans of the northwest coast of the United States prefer to journey in their dugout canoes. These spirit canoes fly and carry them to the Upper World. Many savvy modern shamans visualize an airplane or a hot-air balloon for the flight.

On the ascent to and on the arrival in the Upper World, the shaman may run into enemy spirits, as in the other worlds. The shaman may also find animal allies and some lost souls that need help. The Upper World tends to be the best place to find teachers, who usually take human form. Peruvian shamans go to the Upper World to get help from the saints, who are a Christian form of these teachers. As the Lower World is the home of Mother Earth, the Upper World is the home of the other great spirit, called the Sky Father. Often shamans will journey to the Upper World to learn from the Sky Father or to negotiate with him about broken **taboos** or lost souls. This is a

Figure 5.1 *Shamans commonly use animal allies, such as this Andean condor, to gain access to the Upper World during a shamanic journey.,* (Vassil Donev/epa/Corbis)

place to learn about the laws of the universe, seek justice, and see into the future. Most of all, however, the Upper World is associated with wisdom.

THE JOURNEY IN MYTHOLOGY AND FAIRY TALES

Some details in shamanic journeys seem a lot like the myths, folk tales, or fairy tales that most people know. For example, in Greek mythology, Orpheus used his magical songs to enchant the guardians and gain access to the Underworld, the land of the dead, where, like a shaman, he tried to reclaim the lost soul of his lover Eurydice. The goddess Persephone was also taken to the land of the dead, where she ate some food of the dead and was bound there, just like the Sora shamans' fear. Odysseus—who was called Ulysses by the Romans—made a voyage home from Troy that is like a shamanic journey or spirit quest; in it, the entire Mediterranean is populated with spirits who may be enemies or allies. Like a shaman, Odysseus keeps to his purpose and outwits his opponents—as he sails past the Sirens whose singing drives ordinary men mad; escapes from a one-eyed giant, making a fool out him in the process; and turns a deadly sorceress into his ally. He even visits the land of the dead to gain wisdom. Through it all, his spirit guide is the goddess Athene, who is the goddess of shrewdness as well as war and wisdom.

Similarities also exist in fairy tales or folk stories, in which there are numerous examples of animal helpers acting as spirit guides. The most famous stories of this type are those of the Nightingale, in which a nightingale sings the Chinese emperor back to life but cannot be confined to the palace, preferring nature instead; and Puss in Boots, in which a talking cat helps his master obtain wealth and defeat an ogre through trickery. Other examples include the monkey hero Sun Wukong of Chinese mythology, the hero Coyote of Native American myths, and Brer Rabbit of Uncle Remus's stories, which in turn were based on African legends. A modern counterpart of this trickster animal may be the cartoon character Bugs Bunny.

There are also examples of shamanic-like journeys to the Lower World. In "The Tinder Box," a fairy tale by Hans Christian Andersen, a soldier, like a shaman, goes into the earth through a hollow tree and befriends three dogs with amazingly large eyes. The dogs use their magic and their tricks to help him win riches and the hand of the princess. Similarly Alice, in Lewis Carroll's *Alice's Adventures in Wonderland*, follows a talking rabbit down a rabbit hole and emerges in a wonderland with its own ground and sky even though it is underground.

Folk stories also tell of journeys to the Upper World. In "Jack and the Beanstalk," Jack plays the part of the shaman and climbs a giant beanstalk, like climbing the World Tree, right up into the sky and through a cloud barrier into another land with its own ground and sky. Also Dorothy, in *The Wizard of Oz*, travels to her wonderland by being picked up in a tornado like a shaman.

These shamanic qualities may also appear in other novels or in movies. In *Dracula*, the undead Count Dracula, a demon from the land

Figure 5.2 *Illustration of Alice and the White Rabbit by Milo Winter. Critics have noted similarities between Alice's adventure and a shaman's journey to the Lower World.,* (Blue Lantern Studio/Corbis)

of the dead, steals Mina Harker's soul by drinking her blood, forcing her husband to enlist the help of the shaman Van Helsing. Van Helsing travels to the land of the dead, in this case Transylvania, defeats the demon, and heals Mina. In the *Star Wars* series, Luke Skywalker is like a young shaman apprenticing to the older Obi-Wan Kenobi, who introduces him to his spirit teacher, Yoda. The main plot of the original three movies concerns the retrieval of a soul in the form of Princess Leia, who is threatened by the dark spirit Darth Vader. In a shamanic-like twist, in which a malevolent spirit can transform into a helper, the villainous Darth Vader turns out to be Luke's father and in *Return of the Jedi* becomes his helper. These similarities suggest that many myths and folk stories come from shamans' stories about their journeys. There is also some basic, universal human quality in these stories that causes modern writers to retell them in different forms and settings. It is another reason that shamanism seems to be at the root of all human religions and culture.

Shamanism Today

Jack is a psychotherapist with a private practice in the New Jersey suburbs. In addition to using more conventional techniques, he offers his clients something called journeywork, which he learned from psychologist David Grove. In journeywork the client is guided by the therapist on a dreamlike journey while he or she is awake and can interact and comment on what is happening. Jack has found that this technique helps get to the root cause of an emotional problem a lot faster than his other techniques and helps his clients to heal, sometimes in only one meeting with him. Jack does not consider what he does shamanism, but there are some similarities.

The way that Jack helps his clients go on the journey is by asking questions that treat the problem as a thing that has its own personality and form. To do this, Jack has to use language that is simple and that does not make too many suggestions to his client, what was labeled *clean language* by Grove. Clean language allows the client to form his or her own images without too much influence from Jack.

Today Jack is working with a client named Bill who is suffering feelings of anxiety, which means he always feels that something is about to go wrong. Jack has Bill sit in a comfortable padded chair, while Jack sits at his desk with a pencil and a pad for writing down Bill's responses. Jack asks Bill to close his eyes and sit back, and they begin. Jack wants Bill to uses his imagination to create a symbol of his problem.

He says, “Does this feeling have a shape?”

“It is a ball,” Bill answers.

“Does this ball have a color?” Jack asks.

“The ball is red.”

“Does this red ball have a place?”

“Yes. It is in my heart”

“And does this red ball have a feeling?”

“It is hot.”

The conversation continues in simple terms. Bill sees the ball fill his heart with heat and finds that a vine has grown around his heart and is constricting it. Eventually a seedpod grows on the vine and the pod drops off. The pod in turn becomes a boat and takes Bill on a journey down a stream that emerges between Bill’s feet. To continue the journey, Jack looks at his notes and sometimes asks Bill questions about things from the beginning of the journey. The journey leads Bill to a place faraway where the sun meets the sea and rains gold into the water. Bill sits there in his pod boat. Eventually they return to the heart, and its heat has been cooled. Bill sees himself nurturing his heart with some of the gold from the sun, and then he falls into a light sleep. When he wakes up, Bill is felling a lot better. He feels as though his heart has been strengthened.

NEOSHAMANISM

While shamanism continues to be practiced in traditional cultures around the world, it is now also taught in modern America and other Western cultures. Chapter 1 discussed the beginnings of neoshamanism in modern Western culture. One of the most historically important teachers of neoshamanism is the anthropologist and neoshaman Michael Harner, who in the 1960s studied with shamans of the Jivaro (pronounced HEE-varo) tribe of the Amazon jungle. The Jivaro are an Amazon tribe that used to shrink heads to gain the power of their defeated enemies, but have now adopted more civilized methods of gaining power. When Harner came back to the United States in the

1970s, he studied with other Native American shamans from the Wintum and Pomo tribes in California, the Salish in Washington, and the Lakota Sioux in South Dakota. Then in 1980 with the publication of his book *The Way of the Shaman*, he began teaching his form of shamanism based on these various traditional sources.

Harner teaches his students how to go on a shamanic journey and find their own power animals and spirit teachers. Although his students may perform healing for others, most do not pursue shamanism long enough to become that powerful. Mainly his students go into a shamanic trance for their own health. In 1985 Harner founded the Foundation of Shamanic Studies, and he has since published additional books on shamanism. The foundation also publishes a magazine devoted to shamanism, *The Shaman's Drum*. Harner continues to conduct his workshops today.

Another shamanic teacher who conducts workshops in the United States is Alberto Villoldo. Villoldo started his career as a professor of psychology at San Francisco State University working with visualization to help people to feel better than just healthy. He wanted them to have peak experiences. His interests led him to study with traditional shamans in Peru. In 1984 Villoldo founded the Four Winds Society, which is dedicated to combining ancient shamanic healing practices with modern medicine and psychology. In his workshops he teaches techniques gathered from the traditional shamans he studied with in the Amazon jungle, in the desert on the coast of Peru, and in the Shimbe lagoons in the north of Peru. Villoldo focuses on shamanic ritual more than inner journeying. His students also may work to heal others, but the focus is on the students healing themselves. Villoldo is the author of *Shaman, Healer, Sage*.

Another important teacher of shamanism is Dr. Hank Wesselman, an author and paleoanthropologist (an anthropologist who studies people of the Stone Age). He began teaching after the publication of his book *Spiritwalker* in 1995. This was his first of several books on modern shamanism. He now conducts workshops on shamanism with his wife, Jill Kuykendall, in their home state, Hawaii, and in other locations in the United States. John Perkins is another shamanic teacher and author of *The World Is As You Dream It*, published 1994. Perkins is known for his political activism and ecological activism as well as his shamanic teaching.

Some teachers of neoshamanism look to the traditional cultures of Europe for their inspiration. One of the best known is Tom Cowan, who studied with Harner in the 1980s. He went on to develop a shamanic practice based on the techniques of his Scottish ancestors and the traditional peoples of Ireland and Wales, known as Celts

Not Everyone Is Happy

Many Native Americans are unhappy about neoshamans who work with Native American spiritual traditions. They feel that neoshamans commercialize their spiritual traditions, and they refer to these profiteers as *plastic shamans*. Many Native American groups such as the Southwestern American Indian Movement Leadership Conference have published lists of complaints. Tribal people in the United States take issue with neoshamanism for the following reasons:

- True shamans should not charge for passing on their learning.
- These Native American spiritual traditions cannot be learned from books or in the limited time people spend in workshops. Many of the people who attend these workshops are passing themselves off as shamans or medicine people but do not have the proper training.
- Nonnative American teachers are supposedly teaching Native American spirituality and are making large amounts of money while many Native Americans are living in poverty.
- The neoshamans combine aspects of many traditions into one and create the false impression that there is one Native American religion;

(pronounced kelts). Cowan began to teach his Celtic shamanism in the 1990s, and he is the author of *Yearning For The Wind* and *Fire in the Head: Shamanism and the Celtic Spirit.*

Anthropologist Joan Halifax wrote the influential *Shamanic Voices*, published in 1979. It is one of the first books to present the beliefs of traditional shamans from around the world in their own words. Anthropologist Piers Vitebsky, who is the head of social science at the Scott Polar Research Institute, at the University of Cambridge, in England, is another author whose work is important in the neoshaman

actually there are hundreds of Native religions that are all different and no Native Americans refer to what they do as shamanism.

- Some of the New Age authors and some of the workshop teachers are con artists who make outrageous claims about their spiritual powers and experiences that make a mockery of true Native American spirituality.

Most people involved in neoshamanism seem to be unaware of the Native Americans' complaints, and the authors and workshop leaders, who may be thought of as the spiritual leaders of this school, have mostly not commented. When they have, they have defended their right to promote Native American ideas as a freedom of speech issue. Native Americans are not impressed by this argument.

It also must be pointed out, however, that not all neoshamans make use of Native American traditions. Although Harner studied with Native American teachers, his system, called Core Shamanism, is not based on any one tradition. It is a synthesis of common elements found in shamanism from around the world. Out of respect for indigenous shamans, Harner labels himself and his students "shamanic practitioners" instead of shamans. Also, Cowan, who studied with Harner, teaches techniques derived from his Celtic ancestors instead of from another culture.

movement. He studied shamans in Siberia and India, and in addition to writing books such as *Shamanism*, published in 2001, he has helped make a number of documentary films, including: *Siberia: After the Shaman*, *Arctic Aviators*, and *Flightpaths to the Gods*.

There is one major difference between traditional shamanism and neoshamanism. The traditional shaman in most parts of the world is an important member of his culture who goes on trance journeys not only for his or her own benefit but to heal others. In contrast, most neoshamans want to experience the shamanic state of consciousness for their own benefit. They mostly study for a short time in workshops, and because there is little benefit to becoming a shaman in modern Western culture, they are unwilling to spend the time it would take to become a shamanic healer. Perhaps because it is easier, quicker, and more lucrative to teach someone to enter a trance than to gain the power to heal others, the leaders of this movement create workshops and write books for this type of student and, therefore, they train a lot of people to go on shamanic journeys. As this practice has more in common with the psychological techniques of Jung than with traditional shamanism, this type of shamanism has led to new techniques in psychotherapy.

PSYCHOLOGY AND SHAMANISM

The word *psychology* is derived from the Greek word for soul, *psyche*. Psychology means the study of the soul. This suggests that psychologists might be like modern shamans and experts on the healing of the soul, but from the beginning of psychology, many psychologists have not believed in a spiritual aspect of the human mind. They have thought of psyche only as a material thing to be studied.

In the early twentieth century many psychologists thought that shamans were crazy. One, the Swiss psychotherapist Carl Jung, valued their insight and saw a similarity between shamanism and psychology. Jung, who was one of the first psychologists to begin to appreciate the spiritual aspect of the psyche, broke away from Freud and began to

Figure 6.1 *Portrait of psychologist Carl Jung at his desk. Jung valued shamanistic insights and found parallels between shamanism and psychology.* (Keystone/Corbis)

see the unconscious as a wise guide that was able to help the conscious mind to achieve health, a stronger state of mind, and a stronger sense of purpose. As an aid to this process Jung developed a shamanic technique in which he worked consciously with the imagination. He called this *active imagination*, which was meant to suggest dreaming with a purpose instead of just daydreaming.

Mircea Eliade, a scholar and historian of religion who was influenced by Jung's theories and became another defender of shamanism, pointed out that although a shaman may look and act like a psychotic person, there are some important distinctions that mean the difference between health and illness. First, unlike the psychotic, the shaman enters an altered state of consciousness willingly and can easily come out of it; the psychotic is stuck there. Second, psychotic breaks with reality are often caused by avoiding painful memories or experiences, which leads a person to illness; in contrast shamans seek to confront pain and bring about health.

Besides Jung, or perhaps because of him, there was another trend in psychotherapy that developed in the 1960s that helped lead some psychologists toward shamanism. This was **humanistic psychology**, developed by Abraham Maslow, and which focused on helping people to be more than just healthy. Maslow wanted people to achieve self-actualization. In other words, he wanted them to be all that they could be or, as he said, to have peak experiences. This led to taking notice of the spiritual aspects of the psyche, and in the late 1960s Maslow and others created another branch of psychology called **transpersonal psychology**.

Transpersonal psychologists believed that there were parts of the psyche that were bigger than just the ego or personal issues that most psychology focused on. They began experimenting with meditation and techniques that led to a change in consciousness called cosmic consciousness, in which a person expanded their awareness beyond their limited self and felt connected to all life. This type of experimentation created an open attitude for the study of shamanism. It is similar to Villoldo's work in psychology, which focused on peak experiences, and also led to the study of shamanism.

In this atmosphere, psychologist David Grove developed a journeywork technique, or metaphorical journey, like that described in the opening of this chapter. Grove's technique does not come from a study of shamanism but from his study in the 1970s of neuro-linguistic programming and hypnosis. Neuro-linguistic programming is a method

Figure 6.2 *Writer and philosopher Mircea Eliade stands on an outdoor stairway. Like Jung, Eliade recognized the merits of shamanism.*, (Sophie Bassouls/ Sygma/Corbis)

for helping people to change bad habits into good ones. It is aimed at creating the same peak experiences that we find in other branches of humanistic psychology. Although it does not come from shamanism, it creates a hypnotic state or trance and delves into the same inner world. Another psychologist who uses a different journeying technique in her work is Jeannette M. Gagan, who studied with Harner and based her therapeutic technique on his work. As Gagan says, "The truth of the matter is that as psychologists of all persuasions go about their healing and research many, either knowingly or unknowingly, employ shamanic-like techniques."[13]

No Pain, No Gain

Mircea Eliade described shamanic practices among the people of Siberia. The following account describes the type of shamanic illness that is actually an initiation into shamanism. Because it comes on the would-be shaman without him asking for it, some psychologists believed that it was a type of mental illness. Eliade showed that unlike the mentally ill, the shaman actually explores his suffering and the end result is superior health.

> Another Tungus [a traditional Siberian people] shaman relates that [in the early stages of his initiation] he was sick a whole year. During that time he sang to feel better. His shamanic ancestors came and initiated him. They pierced him with arrows until he lost consciousness and fell to the ground; they cut off his flesh, tore out his bones and counted them; if one had been missing he could not have become a shaman. During this operation he went for a whole summer without eating or drinking.[14]

In the end, the shaman was healthy, feeling better than ever, and ready to heal others.

Whether a therapist uses Jung's creative imagination, Grove's metaphorical journey, or Gagan's journeying, one difference between the traditional shaman and the modern therapist is that the shaman goes on the journey to heal the patient, while the modern therapist sends a patient on the journey to find healing for him- or herself. It seems modern therapists have turned this ancient technique around.

Shamanism Past and Present

The practice of Shamanism is at least 40,000 years old, and prehistoric humans living before that time are likely to have practiced it. Yet shamanism is also continually new. It is still practiced in traditional nomadic and tribal cultures, it is being taught as part of the New Age movement, and it has influenced modern psychotherapy. With this growing emphasis on shamanism and shamanic journeying in modern culture, it is not surprising that it has also influenced popular culture, particularly rock music, films, and literature.

SHAMANIC ROCK MUSIC

One of the first musicians to bring shamanic influences into his music was Jim Morrison (1943–1971), the songwriter and lead singer for the 1960s rock group The Doors. Morrison first became interested in Native American religion in his youth when he was living in New Mexico and exploring the native culture of the region. By the time he became a mature songwriter, references to Native American shamanism were common in his songs. This influence is particularly evident in the "The Ghost Song," which was inspired by the Native American "Ghost Dance," and it is also observable in "My Wild Love" and "Wild Child."

Perhaps Morrison's strongest shamanic influence, however, can be found in his stage performances. He was noted for including

Figure 7.1 *Jim Morrison, lead singer of The Doors, performing. Morrison regularly included references to Native American shamanism in his songs.* (Jason Laure/The Image Works)

references to shamanic rituals in his performances, but beyond that he saw his role as a musician as the modern counterpart to the shaman's role in traditional cultures. A Doors concert, because of Morrison's influence, aimed at being more than a music event; it was designed to be a theatrical performance that altered the consciousness of the participants. Morrison aimed at changing perception; like a shaman. He wanted to guide his audience to that other realm. In recognition of his role in these rock rituals, his fans nicknamed him the "electric shaman."

Although The Doors were one of the first to compare a rock concert to a shamanic ritual, their influence spread to other groups. In 1965 a psychedelic rock band called The Warlocks formed in the San Francisco area. Because of a prior claim to the name, they soon changed it to one they would make famous, the Grateful Dead. The Grateful Dead was one of numerous rock bands that formed in San Francisco in the late 1960s. Because as they evolved they adopted shamanic influences and created a ritual atmosphere at their concerts, they became the one group most identified with that time and place and the one with the most loyal and enduring following. The band was active from 1965 to 1995 and became noted for its live performances in which it created a magical atmosphere that uplifted the consciousness of the audience. In the following quote from 1991, the Grateful Dead's lead guitarist, Jerry Garcia, alluded to the shamanic atmosphere that the band creates:

> When we get onstage, what we really want to happen is, we want to be transformed from ordinary players to extraordinary ones, like forces of a larger consciousness. And the audience wants to be transformed from what ordinary reality they may be in to something a little wider, something that enlarges them. So maybe it's that notion of transformation, a seat-of-the-pants shamanism, that has something to do with why the Grateful Dead keep pulling them in.[15]

Figure 7.2 *The Grateful Dead incorporated shamanic influences in their music and created a ritual atmosphere at their live shows.,* (Michael Ochs Archives/Corbis)

With two such influential bands having injected shamanism into rock culture, it became a popular subject for rock musicians to reference. Today there are numerous bands that incorporate the word into their names, such as Shaman's Harvest, Sixty Watt Shaman, or Shaman. Also, there are numerous rock albums that include shaman in their titles, such as *The Sleeping Shaman* by El Thule and *Shaman* by Santana. It is not always clear, however, whether these groups and albums consciously attempt to connect with shamanic practice or are simply making use of a fashionable label.

SHAMANISM IN THE MOVIES

It seems that in the late 1970s the film industry discovered shamanism. From the late 1970s on, shamans have appeared as characters in numerous films and television series. The Internet Movie Database lists 79 films and television shows that have shamanism in the plot, 53 with shamans as main characters, and 11 with the word *shaman* in the title. If references to shamanism that do not make use of the term shaman were included, however, the list would be much larger.

At first, shamans were primarily presented as villains in horror films, such as the forgettable *The Shaman*, a 1987 B movie in which an evil shaman put a hypnotic spell on a family. Today films about shamanism range in quality from spooky low-quality horror films such as *Skinwalker: Curse of the Shaman* in 2005 to critically acclaimed documentaries and dramas that present shamanism in a realistic or complimentary light. On the high end of this spectrum we find films such as *The Journals of Knud Rasmussen*, a 2006 Inuit-made film about the last great Inuit shaman, Awa, and his clash with Christian missionaries in the 1920s. Also worth mentioning is the award-winning, 2001 documentary *The Shaman's Apprentice*, which tells the story of Dr. Mark Plotkin's 20-year search among the shamans of the Amazon jungle for a cure for diabetes. The fictional 1992 Hollywood Productions film *Medicine Man*, staring Sean Connery, had a similar plot, in which Connery played a doctor searching the Amazon for a shaman's cure for cancer. Between these extremes, shamans can be found in numerous supernatural thrillers, such as *Shaman's Mark* in 2008; dramas, such as the 2005 short *The Healers*; and animation, such as the 2003–2005 Japanese television series *Shaman King*.

SHAMANS IN LITERATURE

Turning to literature, many of the leaders and teachers of neoshamanism are authors, and in addition to their books, there are numerous others on the market today designed to teach the fundamentals of shamanism or to discuss it as an anthropological subject. Although the great majority of books on shamanism are nonfiction, there are some novels and some books presented as nonfiction that are actually fictional. Among the novels are supernatural mystery thrillers and as with popular films, it is not clear that these novels actually have much to do with the actual practice of shamanism. On the other side of this pole stand the mystery novels of best-selling author Tony Hillerman, which are set among the Navajos in the American Southwest and portray a realistic picture of Navajo shamanism. Hillerman's sensitivity to native tradition has been recognized by the Navajo tribe, which has honored him with the tribe's Special Friend Award.

In the second category, fictional nonfiction, there are the books by best-selling author Lynn Andrews and the prolific writer Mary Summer Rain. A number of Native American organizations have singled them out for their exploitation and misrepresentation of indigenous spiritual traditions. As mentioned in Chapter 1, a similar controversy surrounded the books of Carlos Castaneda. In addition to these books, there are others that make unfounded or sensational claims, and readers should not take any of these books at face value.

MODERN WESTERN SHAMANISM

It is the opinion of numerous historians and psychologists that in the 1960s many individuals in Western culture began to suffer from a lack of confidence in their spiritual traditions. As people began to search for a new meaningful spiritual path, one that offered a firsthand experience of the spiritual world, shamanism was one of the ancient practices that helped to fill this spiritual void. It was during this period in modern history that Castaneda began to write about Don Juan, Morrison became the electric shaman, and Harner began to teach his core shamanism.

Shamanism had much to recommend it. Unlike traditions in which spiritual truths are interpreted and preached by a select priesthood, shamans continually go into the inner world for themselves and have unique visions. In spite of the individuality of each vision, there are remarkable similarities in the structure of those inner landscapes as they are experienced by shamans from cultures on opposite sides of the world and separated by vast amounts of time. Even modern Westerners experimenting with shamanism seem to go to the same place.

In many ways shamanism represented the spiritual ideal that modern Westerners were looking for. In Western culture shamanism is not though of so much as a religion but as a technique for altering consciousness and as a form of self-help. In this democratized culture everyone can become his or her own shaman, and many have attempted to achieve that goal.

For better or worse shamanism is now part of Western culture, and the reader who wishes to experience shamanism for him- or herself has many options to choose from. There are books, CDs, and workshops, and the equivalent of a shamanic trance in a therapist's office or at a rock concert. How should a would-be shaman proceed? This book does not recommend any teacher or particular teaching. The reader must choose his or her own way, but caution is recommended. There are now more teachers and paths to shamanism than ever, but not all are equally authentic or honest.

The reader wishing to experience shamanism firsthand should begin by reading and educating him- or herself about what is authentic and of value. Perhaps the safest way to experience the inner world is to practice the Jungian technique of active imagination. This, however, will take further study in books and possibly the help of a trained guide. Another safe place to start, one that is economical and readily available, is to begin to keep a record of one's dreams, spend time interpreting them, and act on this inner advice. This is the way that most traditional shamans have begun.

Whether or not one practices shamanism, it is valuable for what it teaches us about the history of religion and culture. It seems to be the origin for much mythology and folklore, and the inner shamanic world is related to the sacred cosmologies of many modern religions. More than that, shamanism is valuable because of what it teaches about the nature of the mind. It demonstrates that the inner world is real and available for exploration, and it teaches us that we have the power to create health and well-being in our minds.

Timeline

Circa 130,000 BCE *Homo sapiens* (anatomically modern humans) live in Africa during the Upper Paleolithic Epoch, which is the last and latest division of the Old Stone Age.

Circa 40,000 *Homo sapiens* migrate to Europe, where they create cave art and other art objects that seem to relate to shamanic practices.

Circa 10,000 Humans enter the Neolithic Period, or New Stone Age, and begin to farm; shamans adapt to the needs of farmers.

4,000 Humans move to cities and some shamans adapt to the needs of city people.

313 CE The emperor Constantine paves the way for Christianity to become the official religion of the Roman Empire; Christianity begins to spread through Europe, and European shamanism is suppressed.

1400s The Age of Exploration begins. Europeans encounter shamans in other parts of the world, and at first they try to convert them to Christianity or destroy them.

1700s The Age of Enlightenment begins. Europeans develop modern science, including the science of anthropology, which studies human culture; Europeans try to be objective about shamanism but still think of them as con artists.

1920s Psychologist Carl Jung observes shamans in Africa and America and begins to incorporate active imagination, a shamanic-like technique, into his practice.

1950s European and American anthropologists begin to appreciate shamans as masters of traditional healing and for their ability to alter their consciousness.

1951 The scholar of religion Mircea Eliade publishes *Shamanism: Archaic Techniques of Ecstasy* and defines shamanism for other scholars and scientists.

1957 R. Gordon Wasson publishes "Seeking the Magic Mushroom," an article on Mexican shamans, in *Life* magazine.

1960s Abraham Maslow and other psychologists create transpersonal psychology, which makes use of shamanic techniques.

1967 *The Doors*, the first album by Jim Morrison and The Doors, is released. The Doors brought shamanic influences to rock concerts and included shamanic references in their songs.

1967 *The Grateful Dead*, the first album by the Grateful Dead is released.

1968 Carlos Castaneda publishes *The Teachings of Don Juan: A Yaqui Way of Knowledge*, the first of his popular books on shamanism.

1980 Michael Harner's *The Way of the Shaman: A Guide to Power and Healing*, is published, and he begins to teach neoshamanism in the United States.

1990s David Grove teaches his shamanic-like psychological technique, called metaphorical journeywork, in workshops in the United States, Ireland, the United Kingdom, France, Australia, and New Zealand.

1993 *Fire in the Head: Shamanism and the Celtic Spirit*, by Tom Cowan, is published.

1998 *Journeying: Where Shamanism and Psychology Meet*, by Jeannette M. Gagan, is published.

2001 *Shamanism*, by Piers Vitebsky, is published.

Glossary

AGE OF ENLIGHTENMENT The 1700s, when Europeans and Western culture in general developed modern science.

AGE OF EXPLORATION The 1400s to the 1600s, when Europeans began to explore and colonize the world.

ANIMISM The religious belief that everything in the world is alive and has a soul or spirit, including rocks and plants.

ANTHROPOLOGIST A scientist who studies human culture.

ARCHAEOLOGIST An anthropologist who specializes in the study of prehistoric people and cultures.

ARCHETYPE In Jungian psychology, the name for seemingly separate personalities found in the unconscious mind of an individual. They are similar for all humans regardless of the time or the culture they live in.

AXIS MUNDI The center of the world; the most sacred spot on earth; the place where the shaman can make his or her journey to the Upper or Lower World.

CURANDERO A name for shamans in Latin America.

DISSOCIATION A psychological term that describes a psychological illness that is similar to what shamans call soul loss.

DIVINATION The practice of contacting spirits or gods to learn things that a person cannot learn through ordinary investigation with the five senses, such as the likely outcome of a situation or where something is that is lost or hidden.

ECSTATIC Describes an altered state of consciousness sort of like a waking dream; also referred to as a trance or vision.

GOD'S EYE A South American mandala made of sticks and yarn.

HALLUCINOGENIC Describes a substance, such as a drug or an herb, that alters a person's consciousness and causes visions or hallucinations.

HOMO SAPIENS Anatomically modern humans, who first evolved in Africa 130,000 years ago.

HUMANISTIC PSYCHOLOGY A type of psychology founded by Abraham Maslow that is focused on helping people to achieve self-actualization.

INITIATION A transformative journey in the spirit world in which a would-be shaman dies to his or her old self and is reborn stronger and wiser as a shaman.

JOURNEY A shamanic adventure to the spirit world.

JOURNEYWORK A psychological technique that resembles a shamanic journey in which a patient explores his or her unconscious through dreamlike symbolism.

KURAN The name for a shaman among the Sora of India.

MANDALA A work of art that forms a map of the sacred universe depicting the center and the four directions.

MESA Spanish for *table*; the name of a Peruvian shaman's altar.

MOUNT MERU The mountain that marks the sacred center in Buddhist mythology.

NEOLITHIC The New Stone Age, a period of time in which humans developed farming and began to live in villages, dating from about 10,000 years ago to the beginning of the Bronze Age, about 5,000 BCE.

NEOSHAMANISM A combination of shamanic techniques gathered from various traditional cultures and taught in New Age workshops.

PALEOLITHIC The Old Stone Age, a period of time when human ancestors developed stone tools and evolved into modern humans; dating from 2.5 million years ago to about 20,000 years ago; divided into three epochs, the Lower, Middle, and Upper Paleolithic.

PEYOTE CACTUS A hallucinogenic herb containing mescaline used by shamans primarily in the southwestern United States and Mexico.

PSILOCYBIN MUSHROOM A hallucinogenic mushroom used by shamans primarily in Mexico.

PSYCHOPOMP A person who guides the souls of the dead to the land of the dead so that they can be at rest.

PSYCHOTHERAPIST A modern Western healer who studies the mind and helps to cure mental problems.

SAND PAINTING A Navajo mandala made of various colored sands.

SAN PEDRO CACTUS A hallucinogenic herb containing mescaline; used by Peruvian shamans.

SHAMAN Anthropologists' term for a person who has the ability and training to enter a trance state and communicate with spirits so that he or she can help people; the plural form is shamans; in the past they have been called *magicians*, *witch doctors*, *medicine men*, *sorcerers*, or *witches*.

SMUDGE STICK A bundle of dried sage grass burned by Native American shamans to purify an area for spiritual work.

SPIRIT GUIDE Also known as a guardian spirit; the most important spirit helper and teacher that a shaman has.

SPIRIT WORLD The name of the reality a shaman experiences while in a trance; also known as the dream world or other world.

TABOOS Things that are forbidden for religious reasons.

TRANSPERSONAL PSYCHOLOGY Psychological practice that grew out of humanistic psychology and explores spiritual aspects of the psyche.

URBAN REVOLUTION A period of time in human culture when people started living in cities, starting 6,000 years ago in the Middle East and continuing to the present in more primitive parts of the world.

WORLD TREE A large, mythical tree that grows in the center of the world, piercing the three worlds—Middle Earth, the Lower World or underworld, and the Upper World; called Yggdrasil in Norse mythology.

YGGDRASIL The Germanic name for the World Tree.

YURT A traditional Mongolian house, dome-shaped with a smokehole in the center of the dome representing the sacred center.

Endnotes

1. Joan Halifax, *Shaman: The Wounded Healer* (New York, Crossroads, 1982), 6.
2. Mircea Eliade, *Shamanism: Archaic Techniques of Ecstasy* (Princeton, N.J., The Princeton University Press, Bollington Series, 1974), 4–7.
3. Eliade, *A History of Religious Ideas: Vol. 1, From the Stone Age to the Eleusinian Mysteries* (Chicago, The University of Chicago Press, 1978), 8.
4. John G. Neihardt, *Black Elk Speaks* (Lincoln, Neb., University of Nebraska Press, 2004), 2.
5. This story is based on a true account found in Andrei A. Znamenski, *Shamanism: Critical Concepts in Sociology* (Oxford, Routledge, 2004), 62–65.
6. Joan Halifax. *Shamanic Voices: A Survey of Visionary Narratives* (New York, E.P. Dutton, 1979), 6.
7. Piers Vitebsky, *Shamanism* (Norman, OK: University of Oklahoma Press, 1995), 58.
8. The details of this account are derived from Vitebsky, *Shamanism*, 70.
9. Eliade, *Shamanism: Archaic Techniques of Ecstasy*, 220.
10. Michael Harner, *The Way of the Shaman: A Guide to Power and Healing* (Toronto, Bantam Books, 1982), 104.
11. Vitebsky, 72.
12. Ibid., 71.
13. Jeannette M. Gagan, *Journeying: Where Shamanism and Psychology Meet* (Santa Fe, N.M., Rio Chama Publications, 1998), 40
14. Eliade, *Shamanism: Archaic Techniques of Ecstasy*, 43.
15. Nancy Reist, "Cling to the Edge of Magic: Shamanic Aspects of the Grateful Dead," found in *Perspectives on the Grateful Dead: Critical Writing*, Robert J. Weiner, ed. (Westport, Conn., Greenwood Publishing, 1999), 183.

Further Resources

BOOKS AND ARTICLES

Aldred, Linda. "Plastic Shamans and Astroturf Sun Dances: New Age Commercialization of Native American Spirituality." *The American Indian Quarterly* 24, no. 3 (Summer 2000): 329-352. Also available online. URL: http://mytwobeadsworth.com/PlasticShamans.html. Posted March 19, 2005.

Cowan, Tom. *Fire in the Head: Shamanism and the Celtic Spirit*. New York: HarperCollins Publishers, 1993.

Graham Scott, Gini. *The Complete Idiot's Guide to Shamanism*. New York: Alpha, 2002.

Halifax, Joan. *Shamanic Voices: A Survey of Visionary Narratives*. New York: E.P. Dutton, 1979.

Halifax, Joan. *Shaman: The Wounded Healer*. New York: Crossroads, 1982.

Harner, Michael. *The Way of the Shaman: A Guide to Power and Healing*. Toronto: Bantam Books, 1982.

Ingerman, Sandra. *Shamanic Journeying: A Beginner's Guide*. Boulder, Colo.: Sounds True, 2004.

Neihardt, John G. *Black Elk Speaks*. Lincoln, Neb.: University of Nebraska Press, 2004.

Perkins, John. *The World Is As You Dream It: Shamanic Teachings from the Amazon and the Andes*. Rochester, Vt.: Destiny Books, 1994.

Vitebsky, Piers. *Shamanism*. London: University of Oklahoma Press by arrangement with Duncan Baird Publishers, 1995.

Villoldo, Alberto. *Shaman, Healer, Sage: How to Heal Yourself and Others with the Energy Medicine of the Americas*. New York: Harmony Books, 2000.

Wesselman, Hank. *Spiritwalker: Messages from the Future*. New York: Bantam Books, 1995.

WEB SITES

Foundation for Shamanic Studies
http://www.shamanism.org
Web site of Michael Harner and his foundation.

Institute for Contemporary Shamanic Studies
http://www.icss.org

Shaman's Drum magazine
http://shamansdrum.org
A magazine published by the Cross-Cultural Shamanism Network.

Shared Wisdom
http://www.sharedwisdom.com
The Web site of Hank Wesselman, Ph.D.

Bibliography

Eliade, Mircea. *Shamanism: Archaic Techniques of Ecstasy*. Princeton, N.J.: Princeton University Press, Bollington Series, 1974.

Gagan, Jeannette M. *Journeying: Where Shamanism and Psychology Meet*. Santa Fe, N.M.: Rio Chama Publications, 1998.

Jelinek, J. *The Pictorial Encyclopedia of the Evolution of Man*. London: Hamlyn, 1975.

Marshack, Alexander. *The Roots of Civilization*. Mount Kisco, N.Y.: Moyer Bell Limited, 1991.

Ryan, Robert E. *Shamanism and the Psychology of C.G. Jung*. London: Vega, 2002.

Znamenski, Andrei A. *Shamanism: Critical Concepts in Sociology*. Oxford: Routledge, 2004.

Index

Page numbers in *italics* indicate images.

About the Author

ROBERT M. PLACE is an author and a visionary artist and illustrator whose award-winning works in painting and sculpture have been displayed in galleries and museums in America, Europe, and Japan and have graced the covers and pages of numerous books and publications. He is the designer, illustrator, and co-author, with Rosemary Ellen Guiley, of *The Alchemical Tarot* and *The Angels Tarot*. He is the designer, illustrator, and author of *The Buddha Tarot*, *The Tarot of the Saints*, and *The Vampire Tarot*. He is the author of *The Buddha Tarot Companion* and *The Tarot: History, Symbolism, and Divination*, which *Booklist* has said, "may be the best book ever written on ... the tarot." For Mysteries, Legends, and Unexplained Phenomena, he has also authored *Astrology and Divination* and is the cover illustrator for the series. His Web site is http://thealchemicalegg.com.

About the Consulting Editor

ROSEMARY ELLEN GUILEY is one of the foremost authorities on the paranormal. Psychic experiences in childhood led to her lifelong study and research of paranormal mysteries. A journalist by training, she has worked full time in the paranormal since 1983, as an author, presenter, and investigator. She has written 31 nonfiction books on paranormal topics, translated into 13 languages, and hundreds of articles. She has experienced many of the phenomena she has researched. She has appeared on numerous television, documentary, and radio shows. She is also a member of the League of Paranormal Gentlemen for Spooked Productions, a columnist for *TAPS Paramagazine*, a consulting editor for *FATE* magazine, and writer for the "Paranormal Insider" blog. Ms. Guiley's books include *The Encyclopedia of Angels*, *The Encyclopedia of Magic and Alchemy*, *The Encyclopedia of Saints*, *The Encyclopedia of Vampires, Werewolves, and Other Monsters*, and *The Encyclopedia of Witches and Witchcraft*, all from Facts On File. She lives in Maryland and her Web site is http://www.visionaryliving.com.